Prologue
to Independence

Prologue to Independence

THE TRIALS OF JAMES ALEXANDER, AMERICAN
1715-1756

By Henry Noble MacCracken

JAMES H. HEINEMAN, INC., NEW YORK H

Books by Henry Noble MacCracken

The Family on Gramercy Park
The Hickory Limb
Old Dutchess Forever
Blythe Dutchess

Chaucer's Canterbury Tales, *editor*
Twenty Plays of Shakespeare, *editor*
The Minor Poems of John Lydgate, *editor*

Library of Congress Catalog Card Number: 64-20213
© *1964 James H. Heineman, Inc., New York.*
For information address: James H. Heineman, Inc., 60 East 42nd Street, New York, New York, U.S.A.

Book and Jacket designed by Laurence Lustig.

Printed in the United States of America.

Foreword

The study of 18th Century development in Britain's American colonies of qualities eventually distinctive to a new nation becomes increasingly attractive to historians. Henry Noble MacCracken has been very perceptive in choosing as a subject for a biography a man whose career most effectively represents the changes, accomplished by landscape, economy, and society, which made from colonials— full fledged Americans.

The arrival at a New Jersey port in 1715 of a personable, well educated, aristocratic British citizen might well have served a writer as the beginning of an historical novel. His being a collateral descendant of the Scottish Earl of Stirling, to whom Charles I had granted the acres now known as Long Island, his having seen service in the recent Jacobian wars, his youth (he was only twenty-four) would have added allure to the idea.

But Dr. MacCracken's research has uncovered something more important than a source of romantic fiction in this sturdy and ambitious young man. America was a fascinating challenge to its intelligent newly arrived immigrants. They speculated on its history with fervid interest in the multiple problems it offered. Remembering the land of their birth, they felt the freedom to preserve and emphasize in a loyal colony many political traditions of their homeland which its transitory governors sometimes failed to honor.

It is interesting to note that James Alexander's knowledge of surveying led to his immediate appointnment as Surveyor General; and that surveying the mystic acres of New Jersey led to his discovery of the bodies of seven Indian Kings of the Raritan buried in their royal robes near the high summit of Cushtunk Mountain. From this remarkable adventure James Alexander's imaginative and curious mind led him to a spell-bound interest not only in archaeology but in astronomical observations which proved the night skies of New Jersey showed patterns quite different from those which memory told him had hung a starry blanket over Scotland.

As the many channels of world knowledge became tributaries to the glittering river of this eager scholar's mind he turned with ever unflagging zeal to new subject matter—to education, agriculture and to metallurgy which offered him in Jersey's red hills iron, and in the surrounding swamps coal with which to fashion it nearby. His adventures in this area brought him to a knowledge of the intricacies of English law in which he became an authority. James Alexander's marriage to the young widow of a highly successful and wealthy smuggler influenced his conquest of such British prejudice as might have existed in him toward "trade" and toward the sale of imported fabrics at the first flour shop of his elaborately furnished New York City residence.

As frequently happens in colonies the virtues of the motherland were more highly prized by permanent residents than by transitory governors who looked upon their appointments as honors which might bring about both further political advancement and the enrichment of their personal fortunes.

To James Alexander came the opportunity of defending the people of New York against tyrannical activities of a venal governor of the colony. Disbarment by the authorities of the crown only added to his popularity among the populace. His master strategy of bringing from Philadelphia to Manhattan, his eloquent friend Andrew Hamilton to plead the cause of freedom of the press resulted not only in the release of accused defendant John Peter Zenger, but a classic precedent.

What this foreword aims to say, then, is that the young man of twenty-four, after his acceptance as a citizen of the New Jersey colony, developed so many powers in himself that he became a worthy fellow in the company of those almost incredibly versatile individuals upon whose mental activities the intellectual foundations of the new nation were to rest. It is not surprising then that Benjamin Franklin, in reorganizing the inter-colonial junto called the American Philosophical Society, listed James Alexander at the head of all suggested New York members—nor is it surprising that Henry Noble MacCracken chose to write of this not widely known but important figure, to name him "America's First Business Man", and to point out that though a native of Scotland, his abilities were nurtured in those eastern colonies which were among the first to establish national criteria in the federation now known as the United States of America.

POUGHKEEPSIE   CARL CARMER
JUNE, 1964

Table of Contents

CHAPTER I

Scots heather takes root

THE CITY OF NEW YORK was in 1715 a polyglot community of some fifteen hundred freeholders, with their families and domestic servants. Behind its pleasant battery parade stood the crumbling Fort George, with its barracks for the four mangy companies of the British garrison, and the mansion of His Excellency the governor. At anchor in the Bay lay the station ship *Greyhound*.

Lord Bellomont considered it a tedious place for good men. To judge from those that were finally persuaded to accept of it, the noble earl was not referring to himself alone. He died of it. So did half a dozen other governors, either in their short terms, or soon after; not to mention those who were driven to knavery by sheer ennui, and soon recalled. It was no place for the idle rich.

Thrifty Dutch burghers were scarcely exciting company for lively Londoners. They were extremely irritating, holding on to what they called their rights with stupid stubbornness. The sprinkling of French Walloons and Huguenots was hardly better. The sharp Scots and still sharper New England tradesmen cared little for the civilities, and scowled at English placemen.

Even the lower classes had no manners. Governor Cosby, almost on his arrival, had to order his coachman to whip a teamster off his wagon before he would give room.

The port was busy enough, but the stranded sea captains and traders were poor company. They spoke a dozen languages, none of them such as a gentleman cared to learn. Privateersmen and pirates—a distinction without a difference—kept to their taverns by the wharfside, and visiting country folk stopped at the Cart and Horse, near the town's end. Honest folk stayed indoors at night; Bowery, Broadway, and "Collect" Boys, or their ancestors, roamed the outskirts and kept up their merry feuds.

1

Dull as it was, there were alleviations to those who were willing to take them. The little community hummed with clubs and coteries, according to William Smith, its first chronicler. There was a cheerful competition among their churches, though Bostonians thought them godless. "Of all sorts of religion there are some, and for the most part of none at all," wrote the only Roman Catholic governor, Thomas Dongan.

The place was illiterate; a single news sheet, the *Gazette*, sufficed to record the doings of His Excellency and his "court," and the arrivals and departures of ships. Excerpts from London journals were reprinted, chiefly retailing the wars and treaties of the European continent. The peace of Aix-la-Chapelle still kept the Netherlands, France, and Spain in an uneasy tether, while England quietly pursued her predatory way. In America, of course, treaties were of practically no importance, as hostile nations kept up their competitive exploitations, peace or no peace. Indian warriors slaughtered one another at their behest, and were paid for white scalps with the others, by priest and parson, indifferently. Nobody in New York bothered about it, any more than they do about traffic accidents today. Everything was quiet in town, except for an occasional panic over unruly servants, and their subsequent public executions.

James Alexander, a Scotsman just turned twenty-four, landed at New York in August of 1715. He may have merely kicked his heels in the taverns between this date and that of November 7, when he received his appointment as surveyor general of New Jersey. No record remains. But as he then began his extraordinary career of rapid promotion to the highest place a colonial could obtain, and as he was known to his associates as the most tireless worker, the chances are that he spent his few days of freedom in learning all he could about the country and its recent affairs.

If possible, New Jersey, whither he was bound, was twice as tiresome a place as New York province. It contained less than half the population. Its five million acres supported no village of as many as a hundred families. The colony had no trade worthy of notice. It shipped through New York, its unfriendly big brother. Only in recent months had the Lords Justices in London decided that the Kill Van Kull was *not* a part of the delta of Hudson's River, thus freeing its one port, Perth Amboy, to sail sloops through the Lower Bay and Sandy Hook. A few ships landed at Burlington, opposite Philadelphia, when the acquisitive Quakers permitted them, which was seldom.

Moreover, New Jersey, already small enough, was split into two equal halves by a north-south line of division, though no one knew just where it ran. East and West Jersey went their separate ways, most unwillingly yoked of plantations. Over them ruled the governor of New York, who was also governor of New Jersey when the poor man sought relief from dull New York in the pleasures of the Jersey wilderness.

If such a prospect appalled the active young Scot, he gave no sign of it. At his first opportunity, he took the oaths of fealty to His Majesty King George and the House of Hanover, the Glorious Revolution of 1688, and the Protestant Succession. Yet he must have inwardly savored the moment as infinitely ironical.

For the chance to take this oath in this remote and straggling village, in the least of His Majesty's plantations, he had left the friendly patronage of the most powerful nobleman of the day in Great Britain, who had rescued him from possible imprisonment for refusing to swear this very oath two years before. The only explanation he could give for such inconsistent behavior was his ruling passion for independency.

It had got him into trouble before. At the age of sixteen, when he must have been attending the famous High School of Stirling, he showed his romantic spirit by running off to join the Jacobites. He put his training in engineering at their service, as they prepared to fortify the town on the rumored approach of the early landing of James Edward Stuart, the Old Pretender, son of James, late King of Britain.

Everything had fizzled out. The French fleet got as far as the Firth of Forth, but its admiral fled at the mere approach of the English watchdogs, and refused the clamoring prince permission to land with his French soldiers.

The Jacobite gentlemen of Stirling went quietly home—we have Sir Walter Scott's word for it—and the rising came to nothing. James Alexander returned to his Whig parents, thoroughly cured of the romance of Jacobitry.

Then he must show his independency once more. Sent off by his father, after some further studies at Glasgow University, he had been appointed on board Queen Anne's ship *Arundel*, Captain Andrew Douglas, commander, to teach the young naval gentlemen the art of navigation, and to keep the ship's log. He had kept his mouth shut about his earlier escapade, but when the Toleration Act of 1712 hit the navy, and the enthusiastic and patriotic midshipmen meddled with justice by demanding from him the oath of allegiance, Alexander must take it on himself to refuse. And all because he was required to take it, his honor forced him to get into trouble again.

He was no nonjuring Anglican, but a good loyal Whig now,

of the Presbyterian Establishment of Scotland; yet he must subject himself to a court-martial. There was no escape; it was either that or an unseemly resignation. Apparently he chose the court-martial. Honor bid him on.

Fortunately there soon came a reversal in English politics. The Whigs came back; his family patron, the Duke of Argyll, was now the first man in the two kingdoms. Alexander got a chance to redeem himself by reading law in London, perhaps working as a secretary in his spare time, for the duke or his brother, Archibald Campbell, the Earl of Islay. They were only a few years older than James, and already had a good name for kindly patronage.

It is possible that Alexander worked also in the office of the Board of Proprietors of New Jersey, at their London headquarters. The Argylls' uncle, Lord Neill Campbell, had been board chairman and later deputy governor of little New Jersey, trying to retrieve what he could of the Scottish investment in this unfortunate land company. The evil tidings about the great Darien scandal, in which half Scotland had lost its kilt, must have led the worthy Proprietors to fear that their own speculation would be equally unlucky.

At all events John Ormiston, of the board, presently gave notice in London of the appointment. This was in April; James Alexander was on the way to America within the month, let His Grace the Duke say what he would. His independency, it was safe to say, was too deeply rooted in honor to be eradicated. He must fend for himself, even though fortune lay another way.

From the day of his arrival to his death Alexander remained independent of patronage. No mention of the Argylls or any other noble benefactor exists in his letters to his business correspondents in London, or to anyone else. He never sought protection or favor, even in the direst straits. His record offers a most refreshing contrast with the horde of English placemen and American toadies that fill most of the pages of our colonial history.

Fortunately for this quixotic young man, his lot happened to be cast in a most pleasant place. Perth Amboy, capital of New Jersey, was a delightful fishing village, with shipping mostly confined to a few sloop-loads of timber or wheat. The little harbor on the Raritan looked across the kill to the Staten Island kills, and gave him just the quiet he needed to work out his own fortune.

The village life was almost like the Muthill in Stirlingshire, from which he had come. Its street was wider, its fifty houses more spacious. A rich belt of limestone soil ran southwest as far as Philadelphia. Good land lay westwards also the Orange Mountains. Along the lovely Raritan Scots settlers had taken up the proprietary land—some of them of his own name, others of the best in eastern Scotland: Dalrymple, Drummond, Erskine, Gordon, Graham, and many more.

He met in the governor's Council such worthies as John Hamilton, son of a former popular governor, and an official of the royal post; Thomas Byerley, collector of the port of New York, a sturdy radical; and Thomas Gordon, treasurer of the province, and one of those whose representation of improper conduct had led to the recall of the late rascal governor, Edward Hyde, Lord Cornbury.

All these gentlemen, he found, were also of the Board of Proprietors, and almost as new as himself in their public offices. Governor Robert Hunter, tired of the maze of spidery intrigue woven to hinder him in Assembly and Council, had recently dissolved the legislature and secured a new deal in both houses, strongly favorable to himself.

His bitterest opponents, Daniel Coxe, Jr., of London, and some Jacobite clergy named Talbot and Henderson, had prudently retired to Philadelphia, from which place of refuge there presently came an appeal to the home ministry to recall the audaciously honest governor. To which the Whig ministry turned a deaf ear. Honesty for once was in fashion in London.

To Governor Hunter it was the breath of life. He wrote home that he was determined to stay until he had put "both provinces upon that foot, that anybody can govern them, so he be but honest." An era of good feeling had happily begun, in which James Alexander could devote himself to the business of his office. His first act of public notice was to offer himself for examination as candidate for the New Jersey bar.

By his own record he had already been admitted to the London bar in February, 1715. It is possible, owing to the accursed confusion of calendar which English stubborn resistance to change still perpetrated, that he was referring to February 1715–1716, but this is not likely, as Alexander is not generally known to have used one date when meaning another.

In any case his legal knowledge was so wide, and his penetration into its mysteries so deep, that he must have arrived with a goodly store of jurisprudence in his own noddle. He had brought with him for light reading, among other books, the *Touchstone of Common Assurances*, a charming title for a textbook on the laws affecting real property, by a Puritan jurist and good Cromwellian, William Shepard.

Alexander's library catalog, dated four years later, shows an extraordinary breadth of interest, from Newton's *Principia* and other works of speculative science to practical manuals, the best

5

English periodicals, and even the long-winded romance, *The Queen of Tunis*. He was still purchasing at the time; a bill for £50 from an Edinburgh bookseller he noted as "in equity."

With such literate and up-to-date tastes it is little wonder that he greatly pleased such gentlemen as Lewis Morris, lord of the manor of Morrisania in Westchester County, New York, proprietor of Morristown in (later) Morris County, New Jersey, and chief justice of both provinces. Morris, an ebullient Welshman, had married a Scots Graham. He had only a few months earlier, in his gratitude for a decent governor, named his youngest son for Robert Hunter.

Morris adopted James Alexander, whom he called "Friend James," as his political and legal heir, though he laughed at his faith in mankind, and his somewhat mystical search for "the people," who "made the laws," according to the philosophers of the age. Morris was by turns cynical and impassioned, radical in theory, and arbitrary in practice. He had had the chief role in the recall of the hated Cornbury.

The good men of both provinces were entirely of the chief justice's opinion about Colonel Robert Hunter. From the day when he had landed, escorting a couple of thousand refugees from the Palatinate and other Rhenish provinces that Louis XIV chose to call his own, Hunter had been known as a firm but kindly man who actually exerted himself to govern well.

A veteran of the war that had caused all this misery, Hunter had suffered for the unpardonable sin of being a better soldier than the commander in chief allowed. He had captured Antwerp, without firing a shot, by mere negotiation with its garrison, thus ruining the chances of the great Marlborough for a glorious siege and assault in the best Vegetian manner. Hunter had prudently resigned. His Scots neighbors, the Argylls, had got the Dutch provinces for him.

While in London, Hunter had amused himself with the poets Pope and Swift, and written essays for the *Tatler*. In New York he had relieved his irritation at missing the command against Canada by penning and performing the first American play, *Androboros*, a satire on his rival's boastful incompetence. Nothing could have endeared him more to Alexander.

Carrying out Queen Anne's instructions, Hunter set the Palatines at work making tar along the Hudson shores. His partner in the business, Robert Livingston of Albany, had sold the pine lands and contracted to feed the refugees. But the tar refused to boil, and Hunter and Livingston gave up. From that time the two men turned to put New York in order. Livingston helped as secretary for Indian affairs, and also as leader in the New York Assembly. He was rewarded with a new patent for the estate he had managed to wangle out of several shaky deeds and patents. The best that can be said for this favor is that the land would probably have otherwise been appropriated by Massachusetts. Albany, like Springfield, would then have been a trophy of the triumphant Puritan westward empire.

CHAPTER II

A businesslike government

JAMES ALEXANDER SOON became such an Admirable Crichton in business and law that one is almost afraid to write of him, lest the portrait of an unbearable prig emerge. A man so modest as never to mention himself even in his private letters; so reticent as never to mention family or friends, home or property, gains or losses, victories or defeats; so honorable as never to seek office or ask for a vote; so industrious as never to leave behind in his thousands of documents a single letter apart from business and profession; so punctilious as never to write of client or customer, never to refer to his own business trouble, never complain, abuse, or reprimand, seems to have cut himself off from human intercourse.

The exact opposite was the case. He was open, hospitable, congenial; he loaned the precious books of his library to any friend who asked, even his priceless historical records. Though he accumulated wealth, he is not known to have been defendant in any personal suit. He gave to charity generously, left legacies to Princeton and King's colleges, and once expressed his opinion that after a man had acquired a competence for his wife and children, he should bequeath the rest to the public welfare. In short, he was a paragon of the virtues, whose only faults seem to have been that he habitually overworked; that he expected too much of others; and that he was so much of an intellectual as to be at times a bit pedantic.

His sense of history was perhaps his ruling passion. He loved to "peruse and to examine," to set down his "thoughts." Alexander inaugurated the system of records that have made New York history outstanding among the colonies. He collected and bound the treaties with the Indian Nations. He began the rich collection of

9

New Jersey documents that bear the name of his descendant Livingston Rutherfurd.

His program became the admiration of his friends and colleagues. Cadwallader Colden, who long outlived him, remarked that Alexander was the most indefatigable worker he had ever known. The evidence supports him. For example, a bill in 1756 names 333 private cases conducted by Alexander between 1735 and the later date in the Supreme Court of New York alone. Over a hundred boxes overflowing with documents contain the substance of some of these suits. His diaries and journals are filled with others, as are his letters. He early earned a high repute for fidelity, honesty, and skill. His legal opinions were listened to, "as the voice of an oracle," according to one of his colleagues.

Trained as he was in law, engineering, and business accounting, richly grounded also in a good classical education, conversant in his own library with the best of contemporary periodicals and books from abroad, and schooled in adversity by his own mistakes in early life, Alexander was soon the leading attorney of both Dutch provinces, the intimate associate of the great team of Whig leaders that created what Colden called the Country party in the assemblies and councils of New York and New Jersey, and gave these backward colonies their first forward drive.

Governor Hunter; Robert Livingston, Assembly leader; Lewis Morris, Chief Justice; David Jamison, Attorney General; Cadwallader Colden, Surveyor General of New York; Archibald Kennedy, Receiver General of Taxes in New York—such was the team of Whigs that presently welcomed Alexander, and taught him what they knew. They became his lifelong friends. He was personal attorney, partner in land companies, and indispensable colleague and advisor to the families of all of them.

A recent writer has noted that this group humanized the politics of New York, from the fratricidal duels of the primitive days to the system of party rule, that rewarded its friends and was content merely to disadvantage its opponents.

Alexander, at least, remained on good personal terms, and even close friendship at times, with men who opposed him in politics. After all, both parties were now American; the ministerial rule from Britain broke in unpleasantly upon their plans, but inside the provincial bounds they fought each other with hearty goodwill and little regard of their British birthright, except in defense of their American ones. Tory or Whig, it made little difference to the English ministry. They were equally disobedient and obnoxious to the colonial offices that were resolved to keep them in leading strings.

In New Jersey, Alexander was at first much more active as an official managing a well-constructed land office and interior department than as a politician. He secured from Hunter the passage of a law in 1719, which completely covered the whole process of pioneering. What was much more, he brought up all the past arrears to date, mapped and registered in great books of entry that still record his personal attention to a vast business. He finally set up his own bindery for the task.

Hunter had spent his time in strengthening the position of the governor in the two colonies. He had repaired much of Cornbury's ill work; now only New Jersey remained.

These wonderful teams of colonial administration of Dutch provinces, with new assemblies, ready to go along with their governor, stand unique in colonial history. Alexander could not realize how lucky he was to have come at such an hour.

But he gave of his best, and Hunter, a good judge of men, gave him his head. With instant appreciation of the cause of unrest in the Jerseys, he gave his first weeks to field work, in which he secured depositions of the victims of Hunter's opponents in their conspiracy to obtain his recall. The mere threat of arrest and prosecution was sufficient to drive them headlong out of the colony, with their forged deeds and surveys, and their promise to deliver the province to the reactionary group of Cornbury's spendthrift days.

Alexander's second task was to set his own house in order. On the appeal of his friends, the Board of Proprietors added to his direction of surveys the charge of collecting the quitrents in the Jerseys. These ancient taxes, so called because their payment released tenants from further payments and services that had for centuries plagued English tenants, were in Jersey the source of revenue for the Proprietors. For years they had not been paid. The London board wrote Alexander, telling him to spare none among the defaulters. He was to arrest them and get a conviction. If mutinous juries should refuse to convict the debtors, he must get the malefactors transported to England, where short shrift would be granted them.

At once Alexander's independency rose up in protest. He saw himself as an American official, dealing with American tenants on American farms. They should have fair play, and the judgment of their peers, not such Star Chamber justice.

He began by setting up offices handled in a businesslike manner, establishing books of record open to all, creating a survey map of the whole province. He persuaded the governor to approve a law, passed in 1719, which required all deeds to be reported to his office for record and adjustment. Such wholesale reforms were unknown in the past.

The reports of one surveyor, Daniel Dod of Newark, still exist. The surveys were of the most primitive kind. For submitting these to the scrutiny of the law Dod seems to have been driven out of Newark for a time. He and his son settled in Mendham, advertising his departure in a defiant jingle in the *New York Gazette.*

Warning his critics that the land had been "stolen long before" he had surveyed it, he concluded

> "If any are displeased herewith
> Or with the path I've trod,
> The author will maintain the same,
> Whose name is Daniel Dod."

Daniel's critics did not yield, though they ceased to attack him. They saved their fire for a later day. No cause in all colonial history was so productive of conflict as false surveys and forged deeds.

The great books of indentures, many of them, remain in public possession in the Jerseys. So, too, do the minutes of the American Board of Proprietors. It was the salvation of the land company that almost alone in such instances, the shareholders at home came to realize that the plantations could best be managed on the spot, no longer by remote control eight weeks sailing distant. Unique in the fullness of the record and the adaptability of management, as well as by the courageous resistance to destruction by malcontents, the Boards of Proprietors furnish the sole instance of a great land company surviving to the present time, its work well done.

Alexander, the moving spirit in this great achievement, may fairly be presented as the first true American man of business; the first corporation attorney; the first trust officer.

Both Governor Hunter in 1718, and Governor Burnet, his successor, made Alexander their trustee for their American property. Letters still exist, which might have been written by a good trust officer of any bank today, reporting upon investments and discussing the market for government bills of credit as suitable for trust funds.

In Alexander's whole career, indeed, the most remarkable feature of his extant records is their contemporary quality. After two centuries, this business contemporary of Joseph Addison and Samuel Johnson writes like an American businessman of the twentieth century.

Governor Hunter was delighted with his services. He secured

for his young friend an office as deputy secretary of the governor's Council in New York. He thus attended it after 1716, and accompanied the governor on his trips to Albany and his conferences with the Indian nations.

The business principles of Alexander were almost equally effective in the larger province. In 1718 Dr. Cadwallader Colden, a Scottish physician who had political ambitions, left Philadelphia and sought New York after a holiday in Scotland. He was set up as surveyor general. The two men became instant friends. Like all Alexander's friends, they remained friends for life.

Together they reformed the quitrent system in New York. For Archibald Kennedy, a brilliant Scot of a noble line, who had charge of the collection of quitrents in New York, they prepared a great book of deeds which facilitated his work.

New Jersey's businesslike Board of Proprietors proved to be far more efficient in operation than the clumsily planned manors of New York would allow their own land office to be. The province had been conceived as a line of defense along the Mohawk and Hudson valleys and Long Island. The manors were marches— border tracts whose owners resisted as best they could the encroachment from New England and the raids from western Indians. A mediaeval feudalism resulted, by which each landlord fenced himself against his New York neighbors, as well as against the foes from east and west. The only thing upon which they were agreed was to escape taxation.

Thus Alexander's law of 1719 could not be duplicated in New York. As surveyor general of both divisions Alexander became a powerful link between the estranged Jerseys. His authority was defined and enforced. Public offices were set up in both capitals, where records of all surveys and sales were kept, under a £1,000 bond of security.

All existing surveys with maps were required to be filed within two years, whether owned at home or abroad. Otherwise they were voided. No more patents could be granted by any governor or other provincial authority, such as had caused so many scandals. The surveyor alone was entrusted with the whole program of sale.

Dividends of "pine right" and "good right" were distributed fairly regularly, but apparently not fast enough to suit Alexander, who at one time hoped to get the whole body of land sold. According to his grandson, John Rutherfurd, most of it had been parceled before the end of the century. Certainly the freeholders of the state fought heartily for the American side under their commander General William Alexander, who had succeeded his father as surveyor for the Proprietors.

CHAPTER III

A treaty with Indian nations

ROBERT HUNTER'S POPULARITY with his fellow citizens of New York and New Jersey was so great that it frightened him. What more could he do? No governor could ask for any greater token of peace or loyalty. His salary was even voted him upon a term of years, something hitherto unknown. He made secret preparations to embark, but his friends smoked him out, as he put it, and gave him a grand send-off, with addresses so fulsome as almost to arouse his suspicions that they were meant ironically.

He placed his affairs in Alexander's hands as his attorney, and effected in London an exchange of offices with his friend William Burnet. Unfortunately Burnet's appointment came tardily through. As was usual in the British colonial office, by the unworkable rule of seniority, the duties of the governor's office were carried out by the councillor longest in service. No worse mistake could have afflicted the provinces, except, perhaps, the American adoption of a vice-presidency.

It will be of interest to Americans to learn that their Constitution perpetuates this unhappy blunder. The Council, in colonial practice, served the double purpose of an executive cabinet in assistance to the governor, and a legislative senate, the upper house, with an undefined legislative authority.

The senior councillor enjoyed the courtesy title of president when in legislative session. On such occasions the governor was supposed to absent himself.

The American Constitution imitated this mistake, but began at the opposite end. Our vice-president is ex-officio president of a legislative senate, which is also an advisory council under the rule of "advise and consent." The American Fathers luckily decided, after much debate, not to repeat the English custom of giving the council life tenure, except when "the King's will and pleasure" ran to the contrary.

It was all very confusing, and so James Alexander found it, when in 1721 young Governor Burnet put him on the Council of New York with his friend Cadwallader Colden, replacing Adolph Philipse and Colonel Peter Schuyler. The men they replaced were among the richest and most powerful in the province; Philipse held, among other property, the great Highland Patent of 200,000 acres (now Putnam County); Schuyler was Lord of Saratoga, and much more. With Stephen DeLancey completing the triumvirate, the three men ruled most of New York east of the Hudson, and vast properties on the west side.

They engrossed most of the fur trade; all of the greater portion being purchased from the French Government in Montreal, in exchange for English broadcloth and blankets ("strouds"), which the Indians preferred to French textiles.

Governor Hunter had been too deeply involved with his Palatines in New York and Jacobites in Jersey to tackle this monopoly. Perhaps he thought it a rather good system, all things considered. It kept the French and English from flying at each other's throats, at least, and brought profitable trade to both.

The Indians, however, disliked it. So did Mr. Robert Livingston, lord of the manor of that ilk, who traded directly with the New York Indians, and served as secretary for Indian affairs, while leading the Assembly at the same time. His son Philip helped him.

The Indians disliked the Montreal-Champlain route, because they got no part of the carrying employment, and also because French middlemen doubled the cost of the goods they purchased. Livingston disliked it, because he was shut out of it; also, of course, he could sell more goods at a lower rate if the English controlled the point of sale.

On the question of profits, as well as on keeping the peace, the triumvirate of Montreal traders had as good a case, perhaps, as Livingston and his free traders. But from the point of view of Indian relations, there was no argument.

If, in the race for the continent, the English wanted to win the West, the one indispensable condition was that they should continue the Dutch policy of a fair and close alliance with the Iroquois confederacy, whose power extended as far as the Cuyahoga River (Cleveland, Ohio) and whose influence extended far beyond, both west and south. Livingston, who had come over from Holland, and had married a Dutch Schuyler, was all Dutch in his opinions. His son Philip as Indian commissioner witnessed the Burnet treaty of September, 1726, which granted sovereignty as far as Cuyahoga River (Cleveland), and became the source of New York's western claims.

Burnet, who arrived in 1720 with every intention of continuing Hunter's peace and quiet, was immediately confronted with the harm Peter Schuyler had done in his year of rule, by his refusal to hear the Iroquois grievances against his Montreal policy. No doubt with Livingston's advice, Burnet replaced Philipse and Schuyler as Indian commissioners with Alexander and Colden, and later obtained their appointment to succeed the Montrealists on his Council.

This meant war at the party level. In political manipulation during the years that follow, the coterie of Livingston, Morris, Alexander, and Colden were no match for the DeLanceys, Philipses, and Schuylers. The latter, as great landlords, controlled the Assembly; their friends in London were stronger at court than Burnet and his Scots group. The unequal struggle lasted for seven years, ending with Burnet's transfer as governor of Massachusetts, and the appointment of a weakling to succeed him.

For the young surveyor the party conflict meant a sudden thrust upward to a precarious importance. Burnet liked him, not only for his loyal and efficient support in his new post, but as a pleasant companion. The new governor was a convivial person; rumor said he was also very fond of the ladies. He married a Dutch lady, Miss Van Horne, and showed every disposition to settle permanently in America.

Alexander seems to have shared his tastes. He had admired Hunter from a distance; he loved Burnet like a brother. He found an attractive young widow, Mrs. Maria (Sprat) Provoost, and married her in January, 1721. Governor Burnet and his lady stood sponsors at the christening of his firstborn the next year.

If we judge from the scanty personal references to the affair, it was a purely business project. Maria's father, like Livingston, was the son of a Scots refugee, who had migrated from the Netherlands to New York. Her mother was a DePeyster, of a prominent merchant family. Both they and the Provoosts were widely represented in provincial office. She had inherited a considerable mercantile business from her first husband, "Ready Money" Provoost, whose catchword was capable of several interpretations, none of which could have disturbed the surveyor.

According to the amusing family tradition, the affair was carried forward by the formulation of a legal contract, in which the wife was to retain her estate and her shop, and will no part of her property to any children begotten between them. Alexander would provide for his own crop. He had already set up his own shop, Colden being his first recorded customer.

The family tradition goes on to say that having married and discovered a mutual affection, they promptly pigeonholed all their precautionary contracts. Certainly the facts bear it out; they begot five children in the first six years of their union. James left equal shares of his estate to Maria's sons in his will. Maria left her estate exactly according to her husband's division. Samuel Provoost, a step-grandson, had a son, James Alexander Provoost. The children, eleven in all, lived most happily together, so far as this record shows.

The Scots-Dutch alliances by marriage were a most important political factor in the middle colonies. Dutch wives, as a group, proved to be excellent business managers in large affairs, as well as the best of mothers and housekeepers. They were also great lovers of beautiful gardens and domestic fabrics. Having no schooling but that of their mothers, they had no sense of inferiority, and were treated with great respect. Alexander not only accepted equality in domestic manners, but thought it no disgrace to lend a helping hand when his wife next door had a larger run of custom than himself. He related proudly to Colden that he made a hundred pounds of sales for his wife one morning. He admitted that his wife would not accept his advice to stay at home with a cold. So long as she could crawl to the store, there would she be at it, he confessed.

He even allowed her to interpose in his legal affairs. He records of a certain Elizabeth Anthony that he withdrew a suit for eviction against her at his wife's request, though the suit was at the point of service. Her reasons, he added, were first that she was a woman, and second, that she had made a small payment on the debt. "So," writes James, "I withdrew the suit."

The marriage was long and happy. She survived him by four years.

This alliance brought him firmly into the great Scots-Dutch group of the Whig party, as it was (much later) called. DePeysters and Provoosts had backed the seizure of power by Jacob Leisler in 1689 as an effect of the Glorious Revolution. They had escaped the consequences in the bloody defeat that ended in the hanging of Leisler, and the equally bloody intentions of the Leislerites when they returned to power. The colony, by 1720, had outgrown their practice of political feuds, and had achieved the beginnings of a party system.

Colden called Burnet's side the "Country party," a Scots term he had brought over from the Jacobite days. It meant then opposition to the union with England. In America Colden intended it, not for full independence, but at least the maintenance of political considerations in colonial affairs. Independency, in the middle colonies, was chiefly confined to those Scots-Dutch and Scots-German alliances.

Alexander, however, was an independent Whig, if he was anything. No blind partisan, he hated all furious campaigning, which, he said, injured both sides, and obscured true interests. His forte lay in action.

In conferences with Indians in 1722 and 1723, as Burnet's councilman, he and Colden immediately took a vigorous share in the development of free access for English trappers and dealers to the "far west" points of trade, at Mackinac (Michilimackinac), Detroit, and Niagara. The French regarded these as their own monopoly, and had control posts in each. They were maneuvering for Tirondequoit (Genesee) on Ontario.

The rapid growth of the Montreal trade meant the early extinction not only of the New York trade, but of English influence over western Indians. Eventually, it would limit New York to the Hudson Valley. The Albany set were quite willing, and even connived secretly on visits to French governors, assuring them that they could raid with impunity, so long as they left Albany alone.

Thus on the American frontier something more than cold war flourished, though outwardly the two European powers were at peace. Colden and Alexander collaborated in a book which sought to awaken British public opinion to the danger to English dreams of western empire which this involved.

The History of the Five Nations (Oneida, Onondaga, Cayuga, Seneca, Mohawk) is not really a historical work. It is a brief, from a lawyer's pen, arguing for securing and preserving the position of New York province, as the guardian of the British interest in the alliance with the Indian nations. A letter added as an appendix to Volume II is signed by Alexander; the rest seems to be a compromise between the budding scientific interest of Colden in the life of savage peoples, and Alexander's persuasive gifts. It was Alexander who read the proofs and put the book through the press.

When, in 1724, the Albany set had got the attention of the home ministry, it was the joint paper of Colden and Alexander that decided the hearings before the English commission. Their paper was read aloud to the agents of Albany.

For the time being it settled matters. Four years later, Burnet's act abolishing the Montreal trade was modified, to allow it at a high tariff. This helped the economic situation, but ruined the political one. It contributed to the destruction of the Iroquois, in the resultant wars.

The two friends were of opposite dispositions. Alexander's honor restrained him from self-assertion. Colden claimed all the credit he was entitled to, and a bit more; history allowed him everything. He survived many years, his faulty memory helping him to construct most of the past achievements as his sole work. The evidence, however, points to a more generous interpretation.

The immediate effects of Burnet's law against the Montreal trade was the erection of Fort Ontario at Oswego as a British trading outpost.

Meantime Colden's scientific interests had shifted from anthropology to botany and physics, venturing upon natural philosophy. Probably the most learned man of his day, his ideas seldom blossomed into action. Alexander's busy mind could never rest until his ideas were translated into the valorous attempt to make them realities.

This fundamental division of character never affected their friendship. Together they bought the land south of the Palatine purchase in Ulster County, on which the city of Newburgh later rose. Governor Burnet was one of those joining the venture. John Sprat, Mrs. Alexander's kinsman, was another. He spelled his possession "Newboro," thus proving that it was a Scot's "Newburgh," not a German "Neuburg," that determined the choice and the spelling of the name for the beautiful town, the gate to the magnificent Highland reach of the Hudson.

"Sailmaker's Reach," they called it, from its propensity to sudden gusts which so often stripped the sloops of their sail under Bear Mountain, Crow's Nest, and Storm King.

Alexander's partnership in Newburgh became a bit vexatious, with Colden living upon it, and himself in New York. He finally proposed that each turn over his Newburgh lots to his son. Whether the advice was taken, I do not know; it was Alexander Colden, the son, who really created the Newburgh of today, and another Cadwallader who became mayor of New York and United States senator.

Colden's share in Alexander's friendship must not obscure the young lawyer-surveyor's equal affection for the Livingston men and for Archibald Kennedy, another Scot of the Burnet coterie.

When James went to Burnet's early conferences with the Indian sachems he sat beside Robert Livingston, Sr., who was not only a commissioner but the interpreter of the Indians. Thus he learned his Indian policy direct from its principal advocate of the last forty years.

Robert's son Philip, and his numerous grandsons, were all clients of Alexander in legal affairs dealing with the manor and the adjacent property. Two of the grandsons, Peter and William, studied law with him. His son married a granddaughter; his own daughter married Peter. Thus Alexander's Scots-Dutch anchorage was made fast and strengthened on many lines. Mutual interests dating from Burnet's time through the rest of his life made their interests in political affairs very close.

Yet even here, in this intimate relation with the most powerful single family of the middle provinces, the great attorney preserved his entire independency. He not only accepted cases at civil law against members of the family; he even warned the imperious Robert of Clermont that his grandfather's title to certain lands based on summits with Indian names was faulty, since the names applied to different eminences.

Yet it was his judicious consent to the family choice of this Robert's son, Robert R. Livingston, as their party leader, that led to the first Livingston victory at the polls. It was Alexander's political philosophy that they adopted in Revolutionary days. They were, like Alexander, merchant importers and storekeepers. Their church background was identical, as was their birth. But it is unlikely that their interest in law and principle would have been what it was, without Alexander's interest.

When Alexander was in great trouble, Philip joined him in public support. When William put forth his incendiary newspapers, James sold them at his store counter. When Peter, his son-in-law, went into business as a supply merchant, Alexander loaned him the cash. In effect, indeed, they were one family.

Archibald Kennedy, who completes the Scottish-Dutch coterie, married a Schuyler, and bought Governor's Island, which turned out to be profitable. His outlook on public affairs remained his own property until much later, when under Alexander's friendly proofreading he published his famous papers in support of the British interest in Indian affairs.

He was a modest man, like Alexander, and did not push himself. He remained all his life a good tax collector. With the aid of Colden and Alexander Kennedy increased the revenue in flattering amounts. Unfortunately, the Walpoles heard about it; Horatio Walpole, uncle of the famous Horace, secured the five per cent fee for Kennedy's work.

It was Kennedy's pamphlets that first interested Benjamin Frank-

lin in an American commonwealth. Kennedy dreamed of making
Niagara the future capital of a great English empire. He tactfully
suggested that Americans had learned something about forest
warfare from the Indians which even the all-wise English com-
manders might usefully adopt. He questioned the wisdom of
wearing a towering beaver helmet through American underbrush,
along with twenty pounds of clothes.

But above all, he presented the Alexander view of the Indians
as allies to be trusted and respected, their interest to be considered,
their needs supplied.

With Colden and Burnet, he joined Alexander in business ven-
tures, one of them a purchase along the Mohawk River.

In view of his generally reasonable opinions, it was all the more
courageous for this retiring gentleman to join the solitary Alexander
in one of his most daring dissents from majority submission to the
DeLancey view of things. He had great estates in Jersey which
were then endangered, but it took more than loss of property to
spur his independency; a loyalty of many years of warm friendship
must be acknowledged.

These Scots, with their Dutch kinsmen, were friends for life of
James Alexander. They comprised the Country party, the Free
Traders, the American Whigs of the "staunch" school; the largest
single group of kinsmen of business interest to maintain the American cause. It was among them that William Burnet learned to
think of himself as an American. He seems to have been the first
to use the word in any such formal or official way.

It meant an independency peculiarly difficult for an Englishman
to understand. For him, as his own poets sang, every spot of land
he conquered was "forever England." He thought of England as
"home," his government as "home" government. His sons returned
to England for an education like James DeLancey; or returned for
good, like young Kennedy, who became Marquess of Ailsa.

But the Scots-Dutch Livingstons, Morrises, and Alexanders
sought education in America and thought in American terms upon
the growth of a truly British empire.

CHAPTER IV

Two colonies strike a bargain

ALEXANDER'S EXCURSION INTO the politics of New York made little difference in the management of his business or in his public service for the Jerseys. The West Jersey Proprietors, always jealous of eastern preponderance in Council, used his absences as the excuse for an attempt to unseat him. They were not successful.

Nor did his work as secretary of New York's Council prevent his appointment as commissioner for New Jersey to settle the boundary between that province and her neighbor. He became the leader of the expedition which, after tiresome delays, took the old trail from Kingston, New York, and arrived at Mahakamak (Port Jervis) on the Delaware River in July, 1719.

Alexander's journal and field notes of the survey still exist, and very instructive they are, both for the survey data obtained, and the problem of such a survey in the American wilderness. He drew up a plan of work, and secured the written consent of Jarrett, his New York opposite member, to the scientific methods used. All observations were to be astronomical, the deviation and other weakness of compass used to be corrected by them.

Indian guides accompanied him when he moved upstream, and determined the colonial treaty mark of 41° 40′ north latitude at Cochecton on the Delaware. Beyond this point he did not go, first because he had no warrant for it, and last because it was inviolable Iroquois country. The Indian village at Cochecton furnished him with a well-informed native of the region, upon whose authority he contented himself with drawing the upper reaches of the Delaware. Except for the compass direction it is still accurate.

The position of 41° 40′ was given in the treaty as a position "on the northernmost branch of Delaware." Exploring the river from Cochecton to Mahakamak, Alexander found no other branch between the two villages; he therefore believed he had fulfilled both the astronomical and the geographical data of the treaty of 1683.

It is characteristic of Alexander that he left no notes on the forest primeval, the Indian life along the stream, or the beauty of the whole region of the water gaps of Delaware. His letter to his friend Colden, newly appointed surveyor of New York, speaks only of his observations and of the safe journey through the woods. Nor did he gratify his friend's interest in botany with any account of the great trees, the carpet of wild flowers, or the rushing river where he fixed the terminal point on a great boulder in midstream. He was on business, and could not be diverted.

The boulder marked not only the bound of the three provinces, but the northern point of the line of division between East and West Jersey. The latter distinction it retained; the tri-state line today starts from Port Jervis. Its long history does not belong here. The royal commission of 1772, which finally authorized the shift southward, pretended that Visscher, a Dutch geographer, had marked 41° 40′ at Mahakamak, and thus indicated the Neversink as the Delaware, while the present Delaware above the point of junction was known in 1683 as the Fishkill.

It was a beautiful piece of rationalization. Jerseyites claimed that the real source of determination was the size of the bribe given by New York to the commissioners. The use of an old map was farfetched as a boundary datum.

To Alexander in 1719 the deterrents were more solid. Governor Hunter had gone home, leaving the senior councillor, Peter Schuyler, as deputy governor. He was of the Albany coterie, and himself a patentee claiming land to the Housatonic in Massachusetts. Naturally he had no interest in expediting a boundary treaty. He put the whole matter aside; it never received the approval of the London trade lords.

That did not disturb the intrepid surveyor. He proclaimed the line, made purchases each side of it, as his customary fee, and promoted the immediate sale of other patents, to quiet the neighborhood and nail the boundary down.

Stephen DeLancey objected strenuously, demanding that New York reimburse him for the land taken from his patent by the new line. The petty quarrel continued for fifty years, and more.

Tentative as it was, Alexander's line was the earliest example, so far as I know, of a cooperative survey conducted by two American provinces of their own free will and initiative. As such, it was a triumph due entirely to Alexander's independency, backed as it was by a governor who himself ruled both the provinces. It was not a great thing, but it was so heinous an offense, in British eyes, against His Majesty's will and pleasure, that when its initiative came to "his" attention in 1752, it was forthwith annulled.

The real significance of the event of 1719 was the immediate extension of the surveyors' interest in settling the other undetermined bounds of the provinces.

Alexander became the chairman of a commission to effect a similar settlement with Connecticut. The eastern bounds of New York had been in dispute from the earliest days of the English province, and in the Dutch day preceding it. Connecticut bounds had a curious way of creeping down the shore of the Sound, and into the upland hills as well. At times they had started from the Bronx Kill, and penetrated the Catskills.

Vigorous action by the Duke of York and his soldier governor, Thomas Dongan, had pushed them back, first to Mamaroneck, then to Byram River, the present bound. Inland, however, the line of Alexander and Colden, nearly a half century later, was the first to fix the boundary. Even after the king had given his verdict in 1700, the Hartford men dragged their feet, for another quarter-century.

Alexander was trusting enough to take their word when the Yankee commission finally agreed to meet him. He waited at the border with growing impatience, only to be met with evasion. One day it was too hot, then too inclement. James drily observed that a funeral procession had crossed the frontier without disaster. The dead were less timid of the weather than the living in New England, it appeared.

Finally, on the threat that New York would survey its own line, Connecticut yielded, and a meeting of minds was had.

The line with Massachusetts impended above that of Connecticut, for their charter read "westward, as far as Connecticut." The Boston men interpreted this, of course, to mean the South Sea, for Charles II's charter to Hartford read that way. The small matter at the time of Netherlands sovereignty to the west did not concern His Majesty, or John Winthrop, who secured the grant.

Boston's governors had persistently claimed the upper Hudson. At one time they fixed on the mouth of the Wappingers Kill in Dutchess County as an agreeable site for their harbor. Claims quite as bold continued, and became bolder after the discovery of iron in the hills of Albany County.

Meanwhile Peter Schuyler had laid claim to the Housatonic. His patent bore the name, Anglicized (or Dutchified), as Westenhook. A few Dutch families had even penetrated the Berkshires and settled there.

When the ironmasters' war came on, in the 1750's, it was

Alexander who prepared the brief for New York's case. It was he who advised Livingston, in the lack of any British force to help him, to arm his own tenants and fight it out. He did so, and drove the Yankees out of the province. The boundary line remained precarious, however, until the Revolution.

To the south, New York's line with Pennsylvania was no less befogged, though matters never reached the pitch of the Berkshire raids. The Penn heirs were equally determined, however, to secure their own grant of three degrees of latitude within the bounds of their province. Thus in Alexander's time their claims ran as far north as Albany's location. Western New York would, in that event, have been a mere towpath on the Erie Canal.

So far as a surveyor-councillor could compass it, Alexander give himself to the defense of the outermost New York claim. The task preempted twenty years of his life (1717-1737). At their end, victory, though not yet attained, seemed certain. The New York of today is a faithful copy of his design.

His fight for New York grew into something more significant than the mere retention of a colonial boundary. He grew to look upon the province, not merely as "country" in the Colden Scots sense, but as the testing ground of new ideas of independency. For this, its history as well as its geography made it the central battlefield.

Its foundation sustained the concept of a subject province, stretching from the Delaware to the Hudson watershed. The Dutch and French languages prevailed; the people had migrated from a republic of free cities and hereditary estates. A system of patroonwycks, which tried to combine the two factors, had failed. The popular voice had forced a representative council upon the autocratic governors. The people were intelligent, stubborn, thrifty, and realistic, caring for substance rather than form. They became the elective affinities of the Scots who filled their offices.

But in structure the provinces, though divided by an extravagant donation, remained a royal preserve, unique among the provinces. The royal duke who seized them, came soon to be king, and tried from them to invade New England, blending his conquest into a dominion. He failed. His subjects tried to erect a free colony, but the Glorious Revolution turned out to be a fraud, and a queen's cousin reduced them to beggary, from which they had slowly recovered. They were still treated almost as a foreign conquest. Only at New York were British military companies kept in garrison to overawe British subjects.

Alexander believed that here, more easily than in colonies with a theocratic tradition, as in New England or Pennsylvania, or an established church, as in Virginia, a liberal party might develop an American polity.

It would be a pilot project, instructive for other colonies to observe. It held not only the metropolitan location, but the port of entry and the thoroughfare by water to the west where its future lay. Whatever was to be of primary advantage to the American continent must of necessity become its special preoccupation.

It became increasingly the place of congress and conference. With its immediate neighbor, Philadelphia, it engrossed much of the early store of science and discovery in America. Destiny seemed to point to the region as the seat of empire.

The provinces of Massachusetts Bay and Connecticut already disputed with the middle provinces the lion's share of the fur trade, and the right of negotiation with the Indian nations to develop it. When it came to paying for the costs of their protection it was another matter. On such occasions the New Englanders gladly left the responsibility with New York as the "capital province." It was only natural that Alexander should argue that when New York governors signed on behalf of His Majesty the treaties in which the Iroquois conveyed their territories to the king and left the mandate with New York, the latter's claim to ultimate possession was at least as good as the shadowy grants of Stuart monarchs, made as they had been in the years previous to the Dutch surrender of the title that stood squarely in their path.

All this colonial logic was of course heresy at the time. The only true faith was that whatever a colony did was subject to the law of "will and pleasure" of the monarch—by which was understood the profit of the English merchants who sat in Parliament and controlled its boards and committees.

This dogma of the Establishment was never more boldly set forth than by the British governor of Pennsylvania, Sir William Keith, who was then (1717-1726) in office. His views were not published until 1738; he offered them to the Privy Council as his credentials for obtaining the office of governor of New Jersey, then vacant. The Rev. William Skinner of Perth Amboy wrote him that his friends "made it their daily prayer: May it be His Majesty's pleasure to send us Sir William Keith."

This was the scripture according to Sir William:

"Every act of a dependent provincial government ought to terminate in the advantage of the mother state. . . .

"All advantageous projects and all commercial accounts of any colony which are truly prejudicial to and inconsistent with the interests of the mother state must be understood to be illegal.

"Only such parts of industry and commerce as would bring some

27

advantage to the interest and trade of Great Britain could be tolerated. "All superfluous cash and other riches acquired in America must center in Great Britain."

Thus all American finance would be "disadvantageous," while the pilferage of colonial officials would be excused if the predatory Englishman returned to London to spend it.

"The people of the colonies are not qualified to sit upon juries. Judges should be sent out on transatlantic circuit to administer the law.

"Nothing of the common law is applicable in America except such as is specifically mentioned in said law."

"The Crown must keep all colonies independent one upon another. Separated, in other words, and, of course, in conflict, with no direct trade or agreement permitted."

But neither the mercantilism of British opportunists, nor the more dangerous subversion of Albany traders, could divert Alexander from his grand design of defining and strengthening the colonial boundaries as a first step toward their union.

For the time being, the western boundary might safely be left in trust, with the British mandate to New York to handle the Iroquois grants. It was, after all, not the western or even the northern one that was precarious. The present danger lay in the disturbed eastern line, that marched with the New England colonies. Massachusetts and Connecticut were busily at work, eating into the valley of the Hudson, granting townships well within the traditional twenty-mile line, that had been agreed upon as the legitimate watershed of the great river.

To restore this line to full authority, and to set up its bounds by a joint agreement with Connecticut, was Alexander's chief concern from 1725 to 1731.

The dilemma of the Puritan provinces was a real one. Their political structure was bound up with their religious and social organization. They had settled America in parishes, the congregation dividing up their "town" by lot, reserving one lot each for church, school, and manse. They drove out the Indians and "hived out" new towns, which were legalized by their General Courts. Ministers and deacons managed things.

All adjacent land was merely "New Connecticut." Ridgefield in the Taconic hills was the youngest of these. It bordered on the two-mile strip that the province had unwillingly ceded along the whole western frontier, to compensate New York for the forcible entry by Connecticut upon a tract some twelve miles by eight along the Sound. The latter by 1680 included Stamford, Canaan, and Greenwich; the oblong strip held nothing but a rocky ridge, here and there threaded by narrow but fertile valleys as at Ridge-field.

The inequality was no consolation to the New Englanders. They had resisted with all their might every judgment against them, even up to King William III's decision in 1700. Only the threat of losing their precious charter led them at last to yield. But their obstruction began as soon as the decree was issued.

The Ridgefield men, bolder and more numerous than their neighbors, had already occupied that part of the grant lying next to their parish. Colden, as surveyor of the Oblong, as the strip was called, and Alexander, who had been chairman of the commission for settling the boundary, agreed to leave such occupation by the Ridgefielders to be ratified by New York; the strip (of its 64,000 acres) would be jointly held by a company headed by the pastor of Ridgefield, Thomas Hawley.

The plan was ratified by both the General Assembly of Connecticut and the Council of New York. On May 14, 1731, the deeds covering the treaty were delivered by Connecticut to the New York commission at Dover in Dutchess County.

James Alexander had carried out the details of organization. The company, named Thomas Hawley and Company, purchased the entire acreage—64,400 acres less some ten square miles "hove out," as was said, because utterly worthless for plow or pasture or wood. The company assumed all the cost, including Colden's survey. He made an egregious error of nearly 2,000 acres; he had failed to allow for the loss involved in an angle on the border line. For this he had to pay, most unwillingly, out of his own pocket, to keep the goodwill of Connecticut.

Alexander's program worked out perfectly. The organization at the inn of the Horse and Cart in New York marked a historic change in colonial relations. For the first time in history, the entire boundary of a colony had been settled upon a lasting basis, with the consent of both parties in a free and open treaty.

For the first time, two colonies had settled their quarrel without resort to arbitration by a royal commission. Everywhere else colonial boundaries lay still in dispute. Even the century-old border of Connecticut and the Bay State was not settled until 1734.

The treaty line of New York, running twenty miles east of the Hudson, was now safely established as the base. It would continue along the Massachusetts border, though only after a half-century of bickering and barn-burning. It would mark the precedent for Vermont as far as the Hudson ran due north; the boundary would not be fixed till 1791.

Sixty years earlier, through an act of justice, the first settled bound of these states set the example, not only of fair play, but of independent action. The treaty proved true what England's representatives had denied, that left to themselves the colonies could govern fairly.

The gateway to New England's expansion lay open. The churches of that region could now enter upon their land of Goshen, secure in their will to live in a New England way, only giving up their citizenship in a New England colony. As soon as the news spread, the migration began; at first to adjoining counties such as Dutchess. Its population trebled in twenty years, most of it from Quakers and other disallowed citizens of New England, for the New York plan made no discrimination between the godly and the uncovenanted.

There was just one hitch. A disgruntled American Tory, Francis Harrison by name, saw a chance to avenge himself for his fancied insufficiency of the usual "accommodation" for voting approval of the treaty in Council. In the familiar pattern of the extreme Tories, he would wreck the treaty, if he could find a way. He might try his luck in England.

The time had seemed propitious, for Alexander had fallen out of favor not only with the chief justice, Lewis Morris, but with the new governor, John Montgomerie. A careless criticism of his had been repeated to the other party, with the usual result. Deeply wounded at Morris' betrayal of his confidence, Alexander abandoned his friendly overtures. He wrote to a councillor, "My present situation happens to be between two stools, with which I am not greatly out of conceit, rather inclining to fortify myself without the help of either; and like a cat with its back parts in a hole, stand on my own defense against each of them and all the world."

Montgomerie's sudden death ended the affair, and Alexander returned to his active role in the affairs of the Province. Harrison's only hope of blocking the Oblong patent lay in the London market, which was full of venture capital, looking for new "Bubbles."

CHAPTER V

Magna Carta takes a sea voyage

THAT MOST NOBLE RASCAL, James Brydges, Duke of Chandos, Earl and Marquess of Carnarvon, repented on his deathbed in 1744 of any wrong he might have done. There is no evidence that he had ever known even a twinge of conscience in all his threescore and seven years previously. Conscience, as we now use the term, had been invented only a few years earlier by a certain Earl of Shaftesbury. It was beginning to be affected by modest Welsh, Irish, and Scottish folk, but had not yet reached the English upper classes, who all, including the duke, seemed at times to muddle along very successfully without it.

At twenty-three, when James Brydges, just married, set up his journal, he began to preserve his personal record, which reveals him as few men are ever portrayed. In addition to the journal and numerous other records, tens of thousands of his letters are preserved in the Stowe Collection of manuscripts at the Henry E. Huntington Library in California.

The life of this predatory peer has been fully and delightfully portrayed by a keen scholar. If we knew other much greater men half so well, how many of them would 'scape scotching?

He can be followed from his birth in a good but impoverished family in 1674 to his marriage with an heiress of sorts, whose dowry he carefully nursed into something quite respectable. Thus assured of security, he became a hanger-on at court, able to do the correct thing—his only ethical code—and to improve his means by heavy dabbling in East India stocks. No amount of snubbing could abash his fresh face; he found that science was good style, and got to meet Leibnitz in Hanover, then carried a message to Edmund Halley, astronomer royal, with whom Alexander was in correspondence in matters of science. Next he wangled a fellow-

31

ship in the Royal Society, though of science knowing only enough to appear an intelligent listener.

He joined the right clubs, was seen at cards and bowls and the best coffee and chocolate houses. One day in 1705 he found himself paymaster of His Majesty's armed forces. In the process he had learned what to wear, and had changed his tailor and his wig-maker. Of much less importance was his possession of a seat in the House of Commons, the correct thing. He was seldom seen there, as was also correct. General Lord Marlborough and he were soon on the best of terms. Even his too-forward gift of a portrait of the duke in diamonds, which he presented to the Duchess of Marlborough, excited no ill will, though Her Grace let him know that she took diamonds only from the queen or her own husband.

A more serious lapse from correctness was his use of army funds for his personal peculations in East India Company stocks. Some people would call it embezzlement; but it brought results. By 1711 he had £50,000 in the South Sea Company. At the end of the war, in 1713, he was credited with three-quarters of a million pounds. Brydges had not only used army contracts in his percentages; he also made his profits in clothing and the costs of entertainment.

There was, nevertheless, an improvidence about him; he failed to sell out on the hint of peace until too late. The shortcoming became a fatal factor in his ultimate fame; he never could bring himself to sell high, if he could see higher sales ahead.

It was his good luck rather than his skill that he found out in time enough about Queen Anne's switch of the royal favor from the Duchess of Marlborough to Mrs. Masham, to enable him to leave the sinking ship and sail on a new one with the wind. Lady Masham, it appeared, had been a companion of Brydges' aunt, Mrs. Danvers, who now was drawn in to speak the favoring word. He had high hopes that he would make the turn, with his bene-factor Marlborough out of the way. The new favorite proved, however, to be as virtuous as Marlborough's duchess had been; Brydges' bribes were scornfully returned.

Hopes for promotion revived with the death of Anne, and the prospect of corrupting the Hanoverians. Lady Kilmansegge, the plump German mistress of George I, made things easy for him.

With his army profits Mr. Brydges paved his way to a title, taking care, like William Shakespeare, to have his father ennobled first. Though on his deathbed, old Mr. Brydges found himself the Earl of Carnarvon in 1714; five years later, after storming the

Kilmansegge's kind heart, the second earl, clothed in wondrous ermine train and gleaming in a golden suit, with a wig down to his waist, was elevated to the dukedom of Chandos in the presence of a most distinguished company, most of whom must have been indebted to him for the latest tips on the Mississippi and the South Sea bubbles.

They would be less grateful that day twelvemonth, when the bubble burst, and South Sea shares went begging. But although the new aristocrat dropped a few hundred thousands and was temporarily embarrassed, there were still plenty of shillings in his till. He became the prince of spenders for a decade. His wife had died, correctly enough, from excessive childbearing. Miscarriages and all, she had had probably a dozen pregnancies in fourteen years. She died "with the greatest resignation" her mother-in-law had known. Mr. Brydges would cheerfully have parted with all his other blessings could he thereby have preserved a life much dearer than his own. Nevertheless, within six weeks the pious widower was in full negotiation with the lawyers for the hand of Lady Cassandra Willoughby, his own first cousin.

Lady Cassandra was a virgin of forty-six, even in the Augustan age. Lord Carnarvon could hardly believe his luck. In the new family portrait the blushing stepmother holds her elder daughter firmly by one hand, while she casts a restraining arm strongly about the other. She proved no whit behind her gratified husband in disposing her money where it would do most good.

One by one their great plans for living unfolded in the ensuing years. "Cannons," that princely pile six miles north of London, with its wonderful gallery of masterpieces, its superb concert of some thirty pieces, led by a great conductor, its organ for which Handel wrote his anthems: "Cannons," the admiration of Defoe, the toast of Pope—this was how a nobleman should live, in all its tinsel glory. Other costly buildings followed.

There were great dinners, at which you might sit next the great Duke of Argyll or his brother Lord Islay. Chandos entertained an American red Indian king and queen from Georgia— or elsewhere; the Duke of Chandos got a romantic thrill from Indian royalty, and often feasted the polite visitors.

Duchess Cassandra in 1734 was astounded on one occasion to find that Indians had no use for money, and despised it. Another king, asked what most pleased him at "Cannons," rather ambiguously replied, "The duke's countenance."

Mr. Collins Baker's delightful book pictures also an ordinary dinner at "Cannons," with its five tables set; His Grace's, the chaplain's, the music table for the "concert," the Gentlemen of the Horse's, and the Officers' table, for the butler, superintendent, and head housekeeper.

At Bridgewater Chandos bought the manor and lordship, and built Castle Street, two little lanes, and some "factories." In London there were Chandos House on Chandos Street, and half of Cavendish Square with a splendid town house, "a dead loss," like most of his estate.

In 1728 the duke's son Henry made a very respectable match; Mrs. Delany, a judge of such matters, called the young couple "the ugliest pair in all England." Beauty aside, the bride provided the duke with a grandson of whom he became inordinately fond, and with whom, as third duke, the fantastic dynasty ended in poverty.

Deep in frets about his mines in Wales, Chandos was buying lottery tickets to amuse his foolish son, who had just been elected to Parliament, and then wondered why he should be always in debt. Carnarvon might become first Lord of the Bedchamber and even Golden Key and Groom of the State—much good would it all do him. He would always be the prize dunce of the court circle.

From such dismal forebodings the gloomy nobleman was most unexpectedly freed in August, 1730, when a letter reached him from America. Francis Harrison, always envious of James Alexander's success, had bestirred himself to break up the treaty with Connecticut and its Ridgefield farmers of the Oblong by proposing a new project for His Grace.

Harrison was an unhappy ne'er-do-well, who always blamed the results of his own faults on others. He had brought Gilbert Livingston to bankruptcy and seriously embarrassed Robert Livingston, Gilbert's father. He had speculated unsuccessfully in copper mines in the Jerseys. But Burnet, grateful for some fancied aid of the place-seeker, had got an office for him in the customs, and he had even risen to the Council.

There he had officiated with Colden on the Connecticut survey, and credited himself with some of the happy solution in the Ridgefield patent. Montgomerie would thank him when Colden had reported the conclusion of the negotiations in September of 1730.

The conspiracy incubated in the Admiralty, where Harrison sat in the seat of custom. Smarting from his losses in his Hudson River speculation with Gilbert Livingston, and the utter failure of his own patent for 5,000 acres along the river shore, he gloated over a letter from the wide-ranging duke, who was looking for new markets of slaves for his African Company. He would offer instead to betray the colony whose pay he took by selling out the Oblong company and its backers, Alexander and Colden.

That astute surveyor had offended him by ignoring Harrison's membership in the Oblong survey commission, while Alexander had awarded him a paltry 2000 acres as compensation for his favorable vote in Council. Not daring to vote against the Connecticut treaty, but burning for revenge, he painted for Chandos a glowing picture of the Oblong and its potential wealth in iron, silver, and copper, to be won by the duke for himself alone. The ever-credulous speculator swallowed hook, line, and sinker, and the sport was on.

Francis Harrison hugged his secret to his breast. The rosy dawn had risen, after the clouds that for twenty years had so unjustly frowned upon him. He pursuaded the greedy duke that the Oblong would be an easy prey, if immediately upon the passage of the Treaty of Dover an English patent could be obtained, before the American company would have acted. He would exert himself in the necessary delaying tactics.

The duke responded, asking the trimmer what his price would be. Then, his own cupidity exciting his one grain of caution, he never dispatched the letter, nor, on partly sober second thought, did he mail Harrison the ticket of leave, as the passport visa was called, which would authorize the trip to England to perfect the plot.

It was a fatal mistake for Chandos, for an hour of Harrison's society would have convinced the most eager gull that the fellow was crooked inside and out. Instead he went quietly but swiftly ahead with his own plan.

To circumvent the insignificant company of Ridgefield farmers, and the officeholders Alexander and Colden, he would present his own company a solid front of important directors, all men of substance among the City merchants, and all members of the House of Commons. His grant would thus appear a privileged one; and so it proved—Chandos' own name nowhere appeared.

Harrison had informed the duke that on the 14th of May, 1731, the treaty with Connecticut would be signed at Dover in Dutchess County, and the Connecticut commission would present the deeds for 50,000 acres on that day, thus putting the treaty into effect.

On the 15th of May, therefore, with an efficient speed never equaled by king, council, or board, before or since, Chandos' petition was granted by the Privy Council, and the warrant signed. It was then carried straight to the king at Richmond, who immediately signed it. Lord Harrington, the royal postboy, then speeded the warrant to three Lords of the Treasury, and had it signed by them. Thence it flew to Signet and to Privy Seal, with all the noble names attached. At last the warrant roosted with the Lord Chancellor of the Exchequer, who affixed the Broad Seal of Britain. It was done, and in the very nick of time. The efficient speed made a mockery of the delays encountered by most American petitions.

In his first shock on hearing the news a few weeks later, James Alexander gave up hope for justice. He had heard only of the passage of the English warrant, not of the date. Should it antedate the Oblong grant, which had passed in early June, the law, as he understood it, would be on the English side.

But he screwed up his courage. There were more points to law than mere priority. One of these was possession, sometimes said to be nine points out of ten. He set to work.

Colden in haste completed his survey, and divided the 50,000 acres granted to Hawley and Company, into a hundred lots of about 500 acres each. The lower twenty lots went to Ridgefield.

Alexander was in honor bound to defend the Hawley patent. He had given his word to Connecticut. By an alliance of hereditary landed aristocracy with upstart engrossers of trade and empire, the extreme right of the Whig party had secured the powers of government. Behind the semantic shield of a "Glorious Revolution" they had taken over the myth of "the king's will and pleasure." Thus they put themselves above the law, and did what they pleased.

Alexander's bold denial made them look like children who had uncovered their grandsires' dress in the ancestral attic, and paraded in them. Alexander said they must "stop fooling with old notions. You are merely private men, subject like the rest of us to the common law." They could not dispose of any subject's property at their own will, even though it were at the remotest part of the empire.

There is something irresistibly comic about this story of the Duke of Chandos. He combined in his own person the honors of ancestral heritage with the tawdry airs of gambling and embezzling that had bought his title.

The satirist Alexander Pope laughed at Chandos in his poetical *Epistle to the Earl of Burlington*. He contrasted the "stupendous air" of his villa, Cannons, with the proprietor.

> "Who but must laugh, the master when he sees
> A puny insect, shivering at a breeze."

We smile with Pope at the cheap glories of Timon's villa, and laugh at his uncanny accuracy in depicting the puny insect, shivering at a breeze from the Oblong. But we must not lose the real meaning of Alexander's most daring dissent.

He had denied the will and pleasure of the king of England. He had brought Magna Carta overseas, to be stared at by the American public. He had told them that the ancient document sealed with blood and honor, meant that their liberties were secure, even in the humblest pioneer cabin in the American wilderness.

His Ridgefield clients were just as solidly entitled to their mountain lots, as was the clique of predatory noblemen and acquisitive members of Parliament to their spoils, though sealed with the Broad Seal of Britain. He stood in honor bound even more nearly to the third party in the treaty—the province of Connecticut. Possession of the Oblong by an English landlord would constitute a breach of trust that would endanger all future attempts at good faith between colonies. The first honest attempt to solve the problem of westward expansion without conflict must not be thrown out of doors without a struggle. He did not hesitate to take the risk.

CHAPTER VI

A governor turns rogue

HAVING MET THE challenge from England and defied it, Alexander planned his campaign. The English company, by pushing their patent through to Broad Seal in one day, had won the first assault. Caution might repair the damage. He urged Colden to complete his survey of the 100 lots in the Oblong. He got the deeds and records prepared by William Smith. Then with George Clarke, a fellow councillor who had accepted his retainer, he brought the Ridgefield farmers in a body to New York, and in four days got the distribution settled, and accounts paid. He never left his guests night or day, lest the farmers be attacked by Harrison and his bailiffs.

The deed was done. The Ridgefielders plowed their fields and cropped. Harrison was defeated. He came late to Ridgefield, tried to sell Chandos' deeds, wrongly drawn and granting mere tenantry. Alexander's deeds were for freeholds. Disappointed and bitter, Harrison sent his bailiffs to drive off the settlers, who tossed the bailiffs in a blanket, as Alexander noted with delight. When the bailiffs' men started to destroy crops and pull down barn shacks, the Ridgefield men treated them equally roughly. Harrison complained bitterly to the Duke of Chandos of his personal sufferings.

Worse was to come. When Harrison got back to New York, the new governor had already arrived. He was enraged at Harrison's blundering and cut off his fees from admiralty and customs. Harrison roared for pity and once more appealed to the duke.

Alexander might well feel he had done enough to block the progress of the Chandos company, but he must make assurance surer. He sent retainers of goodly gold coins to the solicitor general and attorney general of Great Britain, commissioning them to enter a caveat in the English courts against Chandos. Thus, when the duke came late to these essential officers he found he had lost the round.

Alexander's publication of the whole suit, washing his linen in public, was an even more serious assault upon Chandos' temper. He had always been most discreet, and covered his tracks carefully. These fellows were impossible.

Had he known of Alexander's next precaution, he would have given himself up for lost. The advocate learned by cautious inquiry that William Cosby, the newly appointed governor of New York and New Jersey, was a very uneasy gentleman, given to gaming and other excesses, always in debt and never able to meet his creditors.

Surmising that Cosby was delaying his voyage because of some pecuniary embarrassment, he wrote the governor elect, welcoming him in the name of the Council, and informing him that on his arrival he would come into possession of certain perquisites of office—fees, fines, and the like—amounting to £4,000 at least.

On this security Alexander offered Cosby his note for £1,500. Cosby fell neatly into the trap, paid his debts, and stayed longer enjoying London. Thus the Oblong farmers completed their houses at their leisure. They had entered into possession.

When Governor Cosby finally arrived to take the oath of office, he was greeted by Alexander, and presented with a bill calling for immediate payment. "He raged terribly," Alexander wrote. But as the advocate had taken the precaution of retaining every lawyer at the New York bar as his attorney in the event of such a suit, Cosby had no recourse but to pay; he could not otherwise be installed.

Cosby vented his spite in a petty trick. Buying ladies' articles at Mrs. Alexander's shop, he paid his bill at a time when the good lady was absent, and presented it to her husband, then at Council, for signature. Alexander, taking Cosby's word for it, receipted in full, and soon learned he had forgiven Cosby his entire remainder of debt on the note.

From that moment, Alexander decided that the governor was mentally ill; "I heartily opposed his mad measures," he wrote. And, of course, Cosby vowed revenge.

In due course of time and slow sailing ships came Chandos in response to Harrison's plea for aid. He wrote Cosby instructing him to take the fellow into favor again. He further stipulated that two agents be received and appointed to his Council to advise with him on all matters of the Oblong affair.

Daniel Horsmanden, a bankrupt relative of one of Chandos' company, "forced by his necessities" to leave England, was the first. He was thought to be a safe lawyer, for some unknown reason. Jeremiah Dunbar, the second agent, was an astute but not overly honest member of the duke's staff.

Both men took an instant dislike to Governor Cosby, and he to them. Horsmanden could not endure Cosby's sly ways, and dubbed him "Machiavel." Dunbar wrote back to his employer a disparaging account of Cosby and his henchman Harrison.

Cosby, no doubt in another fit of temper, turned for aid to George Clarke, the second councillor. "He is my first minister," the governor wrote his friend Newcastle. Clarke learned of the wealth and power of the Chandos group, and began to weaken. He finally, with Cosby's urging and promises of 6,000 acres of the Oblong, agreed to turn to the duke. Actually, he did nothing, but spent his time engaging Cosby in other less ominous speculations.

The principal ones were a great tract in the Catskills, a hundred-thousand acre patent on Canada Creek up the Mohawk River, and a review of the county entries of deeds and surveys. He advised entering suit in all possible gores, slices, and other pieces improperly recorded in those primitive times. Clarke, the deputy tax auditor of the province, already had a pretty fair idea of the places to look.

All this went happily along, until Cosby bethought him of the salary paid the lieutenant governor during his absence. He demanded half of it from Rip Van Dam. The stout Dutchman, river and coastal mariner, refused with contumely. Of course he turned to Alexander, and of course the advocate took on the case.

Cosby complained to England, begging that Alexander, whom he loaded with every mark of dishonor, should be dismissed. In the meantime, he held his Council meetings at unlikely times and places, keeping Alexander and Van Dam in ignorance of them, after September of 1732.

Clarke could not help him in his suit against Van Dam. The second judge of the Supreme Court, James DeLancey, showed his interest. His close friend, Joseph Murray, was selected to take the governor's case.

In accordance with his principle, Alexander began to publish Van Dam's case abroad, before it was tried. Cosby was as shocked to be thus presented in public as the Duke of Chandos had been. "His Majesty's good name," he wrote, "ought not to be prostituted to the judgment of a mob."

Alexander's reply was a borrowed epigraph; "Public truths ought never to be kept private," he wrote.

It is no wonder that, as Cadwallader Colden wrote years afterward of this period, "The eyes of the other colonies were on New York."

Alexander intended that they should continue. He needed the support of people in the colonies, in order to encourage the quiet Dutch to resist. Knowing Walpole's determination to keep the king's peace at all costs, he trusted that the indifferent ministry would be likely to recall a governor whose acts were causing general unrest. Defense by publication was his most effective weapon. The statesman outweighed the lawyer in his composition.

Cosby did not know where to turn. George Clarke was no lawyer. The governor had received advices from the home office that it would be well to moderate his autocratic conduct toward the Council and the Assembly. He dared not create an open split in the Council by trying to silence Alexander.

At this point aid came from a new resource, the courts of law. Chief Justice Lewis Morris was Alexander's warm friend and counselor, but James DeLancey, the second judge, was in the opposite camp. The young Oxfordian-Templar deserves a volume to himself. One of the most able men of the period, gifted in many ways, he was by turns jealous, charming, angry, cooperative, religious, dissipated, coarse, cultivated, devious, and frank. All things to all men, indeed, but always ambitious for power, ruthless and unscrupulous. His chief faults were avarice and revengefulness.

No man could be a better comrade at the table. Cosby fell into a close intimacy, and was soon in his power. George Clarke must have been dismayed, but carried on his own enterprises vigorously. A rivalry soon developed between him and DeLancey, that Cosby could not control.

The suggestion that the governor should erect a court of equity in the exchequer could have come from no one but DeLancey. It was new to America, and had been abolished in England under the epithet of Star Chamber, as a private device of a monarch determined to make himself the absolute master of his subjects. It meant that the king wished like King David in the case of Uriah the Hittite, to possess himself of a subject's estate, which he chose to consider a debt. He thereupon appointed his own fiscal officer the executive of the court, chose the judges himself, kept the court private and without a jury, and obtained his verdict.

Other forces of equity, more favorable to the subject, had been used in New York. Such a one Alexander himself had attended as defendant's attorney in the case of M. Louis Rou, reverend pastor of the French church, in 1724. Governor Burnet had set it up with consent of the Council. Colden was the senior judge. The De-

Lancey "interest" had demanded that Rou resign, in order that they might appoint their own man. He declined, alleging a contract of appointment. William Smith, for the plaintiff, had argued that an ecclesiastical corporation was not subject to the law of contract, even if there was one. James Alexander merely pulled out a copy of the contract, in the writing of a DeLancey trustee; the case fell apart. Dr. Colden, chief judge of the equity court, had no need to direct the verdict. The angry DeLanceys left the church, and became red-hot Establishment people, violently against all Presbyterians and other dissenters. M. Rou stayed on, and played chess to his heart's content—his one fault, apparently.

James DeLancey now returned to the idea of a court in equity, of quite a different character. Here a mere governor, no king, certainly, desirous of taking Van Dam's earned salary from him, chose to make the Supreme Court into an exchequer court, without approval of either Council or Assembly.

This time William Smith joined Alexander in denying the validity of such a tribunal. Cosby's attorney, Joseph Murray (later rewarded with the hand of Cosby's daughter), conducted the governor's case.

At the argument, Chief Justice Morris denied the jurisdiction, while Justices DeLancey and Frederick Philipse voted their approval. Philipse said simply, "The king may sue where he pleases," which was of course rank Jacobitism.

Alexander circulated a petition to the Assembly to voice their rejection of the court. The Assembly requested the attorneys to present their case before a special committee of the Assembly. Thus came into being the famous *Opinion of William Smith and James Alexander*, the first great declaration of independence of the American judiciary.

The contribution of American jurisprudence was the distinguishing characteristic of the whole American struggle for liberty. Lewis Morris, Sir John Randolph, James Alexander, Andrew Hamilton, and James Otis were the stars of this part of the firmament. They gave the Revolution its rationale, and the Constitution its structure.

In effect, the issue treated by the opinion was the scope of English law in American courts. Was the whole body of English law valid in the colonies? If not, who chose what part to use, what not to use, what to substitute in an American opinion? Smith, who conducted the argument for the partners, claimed the right of American legislatures to represent the people in making such laws of judiciary. Murray, on the other hand, claimed that all English law ran in the colonies. The governor alone could at his will choose what part he would use.

To this Smith replied that this was more than the king could do in England. What the king could not do in England, the governor could not do in America. Murray argued that "the king" in America was the will of an all-powerful Parliament. In brief, then, the issue was "no court without American consent," or "no court but by the act of parliament, through Privy Council—Board of Trade—Lords of Trade committee—Governor"; a rather attenuated line of royal prerogative, the Americans thought. But such was the fiction that started the Revolution, not on jurisprudence, but taxes, a somewhat easier matter to understand.

The Assembly dodged the issue, merely ordering the attorneys to send copies. Thus ensued Alexander's pamphlet with its wide sale throughout the colonies. Sir John Randolph read it in Virginia, and at once demolished DeLancey's view of approval. He declared that only an American court could decide the matter, on American legislative authority. Alexander was prompt to get a copy of it, still preserved in his papers.

Cosby sulked in his cups through the late spring and summer. He mustered up courage enough to demand a copy of Lewis Morris' decision that no true court of equity had existed without consent of the legislature, and that the governor had no power to create one. Morris sent him a copy with the correspondence. Cosby had betrayed his rage, or "warmth" as Morris called it.

Probably on DeLancey's own suggestion, and most likely with an offer from DeLancey to make the appointment "worth his while," Cosby displaced Morris and installed DeLancey as chief justice. Neither Clarke nor DeLancey hesitated to promise such a bribe when the occasion offered. In the Morris case Cosby delayed from May, when he gave notice to Newcastle of his intention, until August, before he signed the warrants. There was ample time to dicker over the commission.

Alexander gave his friend Morris' courageous action wide notoriety. Three editions of his declaration were sold in as many weeks. Copies appeared in all the colonies, in the Lords and the Commons, and foreign countries, as Alexander exhibited the summary injustice of Governor Cosby to "a candid world." The Lords of Trade, for once shaken out of their complacency, thought the publication most improper and used it as an excuse for delaying their decision on his appeal. As Morris wrote Alexander later, in London "the subject of complaint is not half so serious as the manner of making it." This is the very essence of eighteenth-century sophistication.

But Alexander, though warmly sympathizing with his friend, would not let go his grip on Cosby. He was aware that DeLancey had established an intimacy with his opponent, and chose to continue his assault upon the governor. If there was to be a court of equity, the first maxim of equity was that a complainant must come "with clean hands" into court. Nothing would delay Cosby's suit against Van Dam more surely than the exposure of the governor's conduct in his first year of office.

Thus there ensued another great document, the *Heads of Complaint* of Rip Van Dam against William Cosby. Under thirty-four heads, Alexander grouped the governor's breaches of the instructions he had received on his appointment by the Privy Council.

There were specific offenses charged, against the Assembly, the Council, the judges and the sheriffs, and even justices of the peace. He had endeavored by devious means to destroy the privileges of the other branches of government, and make himself an absolute tyrant. "The governor," said Alexander, "comes into Council and says, with the King of France 'Sic volo, sic jubes, fiat pro ratione voluntas.'"

Of his general errors, the most serious were Cosby's total neglect of His Majesty's forces and supplies, including the fort in New York and its garrison of four starved and ragged companies of infantry. Of £2,100 appropriated, £100 had been spent; the rest were who knew where.

But much worse from the point of view of the colony, was his indulgence of hospitality to the officers and crew of the French frigate *le César*, in the autumn of 1732. On the specious plea for flour to take to starving Nova Scotians, Cosby had allowed the frigate to move where it pleased about New York Bay, taking soundings and other observations. Its crew were given leave on shore, to see the fort and the soldiers, and to talk in the taverns.

The governor had accepted four hogsheads of claret, and others of brandy, with other bribes, though sternly forbidden to do so by his instructions.

What Alexander did not say in print, no doubt out of consideration for his Dutch friends, was that at this very time an embassy from the Albany traders was at Montreal, negotiating with the French governor of Canada for the sole purpose of striking a bargain in their own behalf. If the governor would spare Albany in his next raids on the frontier, Albany would guarantee to forestall invasion of Canada from the Champlain region.

Jeremiah Van Rensselaer, of the great family of the manor, was himself the chief negotiator. Another prominent fur trader accompanied him. It was impossible that DeLancy was ignorant of the mission. Also, at that very time, the French were hard at work

45

strengthening their fort at Crown Point above Ticonderoga, and in full control of all Lake Champlain.

Alexander published affidavits of an American prisoner recently freed at Cap Breton, who denied the allegation of famine in that fertile land with its enormous catches of fish. The Lords of Trade, again indignantly, were shaken out of their lethargy. Within the next two years they repaired the Battery, paid the soldiers, and instructed the governor in no uncertain terms to mind his gubernatorial manners. The governor humbly agreed to do so.

The Lords went farther. They made Alexander's charges the subject of a general instruction to all governors of colonies, requiring them hereafter to observe the strictest protocol.

But with Newcastle at their elbow, they made no move to recall Cosby, or to reinstate Morris, or to order Van Dam to pay Cosby. Party politics kept the uneasy colony of New York at a dead center.

With the *Heads of Complaint* as the talk of the town, Alexander inauguarated a new assault on Governor Cosby. This was the publication of the *New York Weekly Journal,* beginning in November, 1733, the first American political newspaper. The event is separately treated.

A few days before the *Journal* appeared, Lewis Morris won from the freeholders of Westchester County his moral victory at the polls. With Judge DeLancey and his fellow "Barons of the Exchequer," as Alexander called them—quite legally, but with more than a hint of satire—arrayed among the court party at the election of an assemblyman, and looking on as the poll progressed, the voters returned Morris by a handsome majority of the unterrified inhabitants.

The opposing candidate was a missioner of the Society for the Propagation of the Gospel in Foreign Parts (SPG), with the weight of the Establishment behind him. The Episcopal Church at Eastchester common saw its minister defeated. It was for Alexander a glorious victory.

DeLancey was furious, and more furious still at the delightful piece of reporting of the election in Alexander's *Journal.* He went before the New York grand jury a few weeks later, telling the jury that the *Journal* was printing libelous stuff, and ordering them to indict the printer, John Peter Zenger. They took no action.

Whatever plans for a more direct attack upon Alexander DeLancey may have had in the early weeks of 1734, they were interrupted by the misadventures of Francis Harrison. His commission as a sort of provincial sheriff had been given him by Cosby, no doubt to keep him from making further trouble in London. Cosby had given him the supervision of two other agents, John Alsop and Edward Blagg, in a search among the land records for vacant lands that might be appropriated by the governor. It is not improbable that the old baboon, as the *Journal* called him, resenting this new and degrading job, thought of approaching Alexander's party with a view to a compromise between Chandos and the Oblong.

At any rate, "the affair of Blagg" was discussed in an Oblong conference. Nothing came of it. Daniel Horsmanden, an equally tricky placeman, seems also to have thought of using Blagg.

Harrison's journeys to and fro on Cosby's business were also contemptuously referred to by Alexander as the rutting outruns and slinkings back to the kennel of a "spaniel." The poor dog returned to his master in December, and soon had his own affairs to worry about.

William Truesdell of Norwalk, a poor fellow with a wife and six young children, had acted as a sort of bailiff or informer for Harrison in previous years. In the summer of 1732, Harrison employed the man to provoke the riots at Ridgefield. For three weeks a gang of some twenty men entered upon the newly established lands, tore down fences, drove off the cattle, pulled down the barns, and wrecked at least one house. They were finally driven off by the Ridgefield men, the same, no doubt, who treated Harrison so roughly. Truesdell applied to Harrison for his wages.

Through his son, who worked in the post office, Harrison was enabled to open and read some letters that had been posted in Boston for Truesdell. He learned that a certain Joseph Welden, a Bay merchant, had given Truesdell credit for some purchases and was writing to learn when he might expect payment. This gave the shifty fox his inspiration. Forging a writ and signing Welden's name, he sent it to the New York sheriff. At the same time, he invited Truesdell to meet him at an inn. When Truesdell arrived, Harrison found the beer unpalatable. Moving to another inn, he sent word back to Truesdell to follow him where the ale would be better. When the unsuspecting farmer came, he was arrested by a sheriff and there his Judas, Harrison, found him in the toils.

Truesdell lay nine weeks in jail on a charge of £200. He got word to Alexander that if he could be bailed out, he would make a clear breast of his work. The attorney planned with his usual thoroughness. Having visited Truesdell and put faith in his story, he laid the affair before the Oblong meeting, and obtained a vote of financial support. Then he secured the bail.

Truesdell returned to Norwalk, where he found his family evicted by the cruel trickster. His friends told him they had had letters from Harrison offering to prosecute suits for them if they would plead against Truesdell.

One day in August, 1733, Truesdell met Welden at Norwalk. The merchant was on his way to sail for London from New York, but he was indignant at what he heard and readily agreed to help.

In the following December, the suit came to trial. Alexander, meanwhile, exhibited Welden's affidavit in open court. Welden had sent word to Harrison to meet him, if he dared. Harrison went fishing.

The case was put over till the next term, on the ground that Blagg could not attend. This time Harrison had persuaded David Jamison, the dean of the New York bar and a high-minded man, who had been displaced by Morris, to act as his attorney. Joseph Worrall, one of Cosby's secretaries, was his assistant.

Alexander overrode all opposition. Welden was there to swear he had never even met Harrison, never intended to sue Truesdell. Harrison was indicted by a second grand jury in May on a suit for £150 for false imprisonment; damages of £68 were assessed by the jury, with £30 costs.

Meantime James Brown of Ridgefield had paid off Truesdell's petty debts, and restored his home to the family. So poor was Truesdell that he had sold the silver buckles from his shoes, and even his seal ring. Nothing could have been more degrading to a poor bailiff.

William Smith agreed to take out writs for a second suit at law, charging the more serious crimes of forgery and conspiracy.

With this hanging over his head, and the relentless Alexander waiting to meet him at court, Francis Harrison went completely to pieces. He committed an act of the purest folly, the desperate device of a panicking man.

On February 1, 1734, a few days before the trial, Mr. and Mrs. Alexander entertained in New York their friends, Mr. and Mrs. John Hamilton, Miss Anne de Peyster, and John Sprat. The Hamiltons were of Jersey; John was a councillor and in later years

As farewells were being said on the stoop, one of the guests lieutenant governor of New Jersey. The others were near relatives. picked up a letter. It was given to James Alexander, who perused the superscription, remarking that the handwriting resembled Harrison's. The others agreed. James then opened the letter. It was an anonymous threat, from one who had been a gentleman, but was now in need. Addressed to Mrs. Alexander, it instructed her to deposit a large sum of money behind her cellar door, and to remove her whole family from the city. Otherwise, she and all of them would be destroyed by the firing of the house, with their escape prevented.

Alexander moved in for the kill. He took down the depositions of his guests. Next day they were attested before Mayor Lurting of the city. Alexander, though urged against the step by John Hamilton, immediately published the letter and a full account in his paper on February 4th.

There ensued a wide-open scandal and controversy. The obsequious Council defended Cosby's man by declaring the incendiary letter a double forgery, cunningly designed to discredit the governor. The attestants were subpoenaed before a committee of the Council, but refused to attend until they knew the terms. Alexander agreed to attend, but took the precaution of avoiding assassination by enlisting a band of gentlemen, who volunteered to escort him, and who awaited the Council in an adjoining room at the appointed tavern. The Council stayed at home.

Francis Harrison fell one step further down the ladder of degradation. He published a feeble defense, in the form of a letter to the mayor. Alexander seized his chance. In a *Vindication* of himself and Smith, he first defended himself against the charge of forging the letter to defame his colleague in the Council, then printed a full account of Harrison's treachery in the case of Truesdell.

In the fall of 1734 Lewis Morris sailed for England; as the agent of the Oblong company, he was given £100 for his expenses. At a conference with Lewis Morris, Jr., Alexander prepared an agenda. The justice was to work for the removal of Harrison and Horsmanden, a three-year term for the Assembly, the governor's abstention from the Council when it sat in a legislative capacity, and the grant of new charters to Albany and New York. These were, of course, Alexander's constitutional principles. Morris also took with him a complete portfolio of documents, which the Duke of Chandos perused at the office of the Board of Trade. Of Alexander's *Vindication,* which the duke most attentively read, Chandos wrote,

"Of all the papers I have seen, it is, next to the report which was drawn up by Aislabie and Lord Bingley, in Queen Anne's time, against Sir Henry Mukworth, the closest and most severe I have read, and if it does not prove Harrison to be a perfect hypocrite, it shows however, he has been to blame in this affair of Truesdell, and proves very fully themselves, Alexander and Smith, two of the most artful and dangerous men living."

He added, to his friend,

"I believe you will think it very shrewdly wrote, and that they are a couple of people one would not care to have as enemies."

The duke's ardor for the Oblong acres had been very sensibly cooling for some time. Over and over again he wished that he had never heard of the place, which had brought only ridicule to him, and losses to his friends who would never trust him again.

He was not the only man in London to suffer disillusion that year. Chief Justice Lewis Morris could get nowhere on his mission of thwarting "Machiavel" Cosby's supporters in the ministry. As his son, Robert Hunter Morris, remarked, "This is the land of promises." The justice wrote discouraging reports to Alexander, who never faltered in his courageous hopes. Morris put his finger on the basic weakness of the whole outlook of the fashionable gentlemen who held then the destinies of the kingdom.

What chance had Alexander for justice in a government where "the thing complained of is nowhere near so criminal as the manner of complaint in the injured?" Morris and Alexander, by attempting through the publication of their case to rouse public opinion in their favor, had committed the unforgivable offense of giving away the sacred code of gentility.

The Walpole regime might be grinding to a halt; it still pretended that peace and harmony prevailed in His Majesty's dominions. Thus Morris dashed Alexander's hopes with his discovery.

"Alas, my friend, parliaments are parliaments everywhere, here as well as with us. . . . The pranks of a plantation governor are sport to them but death to us. . . ."

Fortunately for Morris, a new spirit of reform was rising, that refused to laugh away the dangerous follies of public officials. After two years of waiting upon great lords and their mistresses, Alexander's embittered friend won a halfway acquittal from Governor Cosby's charges against him, and a halfway commitment to compensation with some other office. In 1738 Morris became the first governor of New Jersey on an independent footing.

CHAPTER VII

A political journal stirs public opinion

THERE WAS NO PRECEDENT for a political newspaper in America. The *New York Gazette* was a mere court calendar and trade sheet. Franklin's *Pennsylvania Gazette* published essays, but carefully avoided political issues. Boston had jailed Franklin's brother for an affront to the clergy; he had no enthusiasm at the time for a like fate.

In launching a political journal Alexander would have to launch a direct offensive against the king's representative. He risked not only his own position, but that of his family and friends, their fortunes on sea and land. For little more than this, Jack Leisler had been hanged. Treason, he knew well, was a very elastic word.

John Peter Zenger, a "poor" Palatine and a printer, suddenly announced the appearance of the *New York Weekly Journal* on November 5, 1733. Within two days everybody who was anybody knew that James Alexander had a new job. There was no need of a sign manual; his style was stamped on every page.

Alexander looked on journalism as a type of satire. He announced his intention of letting the evildoer feel the lash of scorn. His account of Colonel Morris' success at the Eastchester polls could not have been improved by Defoe. The cavalcade of the lords of the manors and their tenants across the autumn woods; the scene at the common; the unjust sheriff and the craven opponent; the victory banquet at the Black Horse—the whole color and feel of the time is there, mingled with jibes and nudges for the knowing ones.

Zenger and Alexander had long been friends. When, five years before, there was a good prospect of a municipal library, Alexander had suggested Zenger as custodian of the volumes. As a book and newspaper dealer, Zenger found Alexander his most liberal patron. The scheme had fallen through after Governor Burnet had left; but Zenger's gratitude remained. He would gladly do a good turn for a patron who treated a mere printer as his friend.

Alexander handsomely acknowledged his indebtedness for material to John Trenchard and Thomas Gordon, the liveliest pamphleteers of his day. They purveyed the ideas of the Puritan reformers of the English constitution, but did not improve on them. The American altered them at will, "tacking" fragments together, omitting digressions and ornament, and in general greatly improved his sources. He was, however, by no means restricted to them. His letters on freedom of speech and press, printed by Franklin in his *Gazette* and by Zenger (in part) the following year, prove that he was well read in Algernon Sydney's republican ideas. He undoubtedly knew that Sydney had contributed greatly to William Penn's Pennsylvanian constitution. His own enthusiasm for reform of legal fees may have come from Penn, as may his concept of a powerful council; it was a favorite idea of other theorists of the time.

His deep sense of the breach of trust or confidence as the worst of crimes may have come direct from Cromwell. With him he shared an admiration for the Dutch Republic; with Milton he wanted the Council to be exclusively of the best men, chosen for life. He knew Vane well. He probably owed to Sir James Harrington's *Oceana* the idea of balance of limited powers, though he gave to it an engineer's concept of the mutual checking of any one absolute authority by the other two branches of government. The engineer's training was, of course, supplemented by his own experience in office as councillor and assemblyman. He knew well how governor, Council, and Assembly constantly competed for power, and added to his concept of "the king" the power of hearing appeals, as head of the Lords Justices. His sketch of the powers resembles Harrington's; "the senate proposing, the people resolving, the magistracy executing."

Thus thirty years before John Adams, an American statesman drank deeply at the great fountainhead of democracy, the British Commonwealth.

Like Harrington, too, he probably said, "If there must be a king, let him be bridled by law, like anyone else." But he never went further than the myth. "The king" was the final parliamentary power, entrusted to a chief magistrate who might be dispensed with at the people's will. In this he was rather the fellow-country-man of the Presbyterian Rutherfurd, and his *Lex Rex* (*Law is King*), which made a great stir in 1703, when Alexander was in school.

With Harrington also Alexander shared a curiosity about other constitutions in Europe. As Harrington learned much from Venice, so Alexander commended to New Yorkers the perusal of Molesworth's account of the revolution in Denmark, where the people's assembly had achieved great reforms.

In his personal approach Alexander seems to have most closely resembled John Selden, whose legal skill, distrust of religiosity, skepticism of kingship, sense of history, collecting of records and old books, and strong constitutionalism were also Alexander's leading traits. An Englishman would best understand Alexander as the Selden of America.

Alexander never advocated independence of Great Britain. But his deliberate choice of subjects for the *Journal* was certainly tendentious. A notable instance was the reference in three issues to the recent history of Denmark's revolution, by Robert Molesworth, referred to above. His theme was the uprising of the merchant class, which deprived the king and the nobility of their power, set the serfs and peasants free, opened public schools, placed all land under equitable systems of taxation, and protected trade. Militarism was reduced, Denmark adopting the old Dutch saying that it was more desirable to rule by love than by force. It was not difficult to read between the lines, that Alexander thought a little revolution of this kind would do no harm either to England or to America. Thomas Jefferson would have approved the sentiment.

So the *Journal* kept on its rash and fearless way. No. 7, one of the four issues which Cosby's compliant Council ordered to be "burnt by the common hangman upon the Bowling Green," accused the governor of ordering Samuel Baker, a worthy merchant and member of a committee to choose an agent to represent the New York merchants in London, to appoint Francis Harrison, Cosby's underling, "or he would not draw a warrant to pay him."

On and on went the *Journal*. It gave the aroused New Yorkers a satirical zoo of their own. It was complete with catamount, monkey, and baboon, "old hackney," "bald-faced gelding," spaniel, fox, and geese.

They were introduced to Aminadab Downright and Ebenezer Holdfast, good Quakers in their shovel hats, asking why they, too, should not be freeholders. They read a letter from Timothy Wheelwright and his worker friends: Shuttle the Weaver, Strip the Tanner, Plane the Joiner, Rub the Currier, Tar the Boatman,

Smallrent the Landlord, and Slush the Chandler, who met over a bowl of blackstrap, and asked why they who were already poor enough should be getting poorer. "Eating and drinking," they had heard, "works wonders."

A word was said for the liberal landlords, too, who believed in free enterprise. Colonel Quondam of Queens County was heard to remark, "who dares oppress my friends?"

In the second year came a series of articles alternating with his polemics on the ideals of life, liberty, and the pursuit of happiness. Four leaders were given to happiness. Life and liberty were continuing themes.

The insistence upon liberty in every page of the *Journal* must be equated with the conditions of the times. Slaves were on the streets, bound men and women confined in their employment, prisons filled with debtors. What liberty had the poor with no welfare of any kind? Every kind of liberty, to use Alexander's word, was precarious.

Intolerance was seldom a New York failing, though it shared rather unwillingly in slavery, the great stain of the eighteenth-century Enlightenment. Alexander's own colleagues in the *Journal's* campaign were a German printer, a Palatine farmer from upriver, a Ridgefield ne'er-do-well, a Dutch official, a rural politician. In the mass of papers of Alexander's devoted to his *Journal* period are also French poems, Dutch dialectal tavern talk, Negro dialect pieces, while "Jack Frenchman" is a contributor in the *Journal* itself.

These were not mere appeals to mob misrule; Alexander knew and liked ordinary uneducated people. He emphasized duties and obligations and bore down hard on justice as the standard of life. He had no use for what he called a kind of modesty in citizens, really laziness, or "accidie" as Chaucer called it; the melancholy admission that things are all wrong; but what can be done about them? He wrote a letter denouncing such public enemies.

In his zeal to make Zenger's *Journal* a political power, Alexander broke away from the traditional makeup. The polemical essay was printed in large type, pushing European news off the front page. News of sensational or partisan concern was featured. Truesdell was given his full day in court. Harrison's tortuous path could be followed to its fall. Trials were given extended coverage. Saucy notes and pasquils filled the pages, where arrivals and sailings were reported. Sejanus debated with Publicola, but Timothy Standby and many other tendentious names were signed to squibs. The Goshen manifesto was signed by its threescore and ten members. Courts were reported much more fully than was considered proper by the Lords of Trade. Dr. Colden was shocked by many items, and wrote in after days that such vulgarity must have been regretted in the cooler moods of the perpetrators.

The mood of the editor varied from fortitude to exultation. Incessant repetition of the word "liberty" hammered home the basis of the enterprise. He pounded away at Cosby's threat to liberty until—to use his own expression for it—"the minds of the people became riveted upon it." Writing every day on the brink of suppression, Alexander fought behind the shield of Addison, Trenchard, Gordon, and many legal authorities. Foreseeing his own possible arrest, he prepared a manuscript list of appointments, credentials, and honors such as the "freedom" of New York City, his reward for his work on the new city charter. He "retired to the country" to write freely.

"He has trod very near treason," wrote George Clarke to the Lords of Trade, and he was quite right. It is difficult, indeed, to match in history such a stirring up of popular resentment, which came so close to rebellion, and then ran off in purely legal channels. One thinks of Cicero and his friends against Catiline, of the Gracchi and the *plebs*, of the French Convention, the Long Parliament.

Nothing just like it comes to mind. It was led by a lawyer, who refused to entertain bitterness or revengeful thoughts, and worked skillfully within a frame of reference that always included the London with which he was in touch.

The *Journal* had its weakness. It planted mischief, but did not provide or even suggest organization. In party and practical politics, Alexander was an unskilled novice. He trusted to mental conviction alone, and consequently he fought a lone fight, aided not by lifelong friends, but by parties which thought to profit by going with him for the time.

He had no Samuel Adams to promote committees of correspondence, no Aaron Burr to capture a Tammany Hall and make it master of a city for a century and a half, no Van Buren with a statewide regency, and party friends in every state.

The *Journal* took root only for a few years, scattered some seeds, and withered. Its history remained vivid enough until the Revolutionary generation had passed. It then entered the unread but none the less permanent record of the time. Today, under the threat of decay or destruction of free institutions, it takes on a new significance. James Alexander's name may again become a part of our national heritage.

He was the first American to challenge the ruling power, represented in the chief justice of the colony, on the issue of equality under law. As basis for the charge of libel, Justice DeLancey chose two articles in Nos. 13 and 23, which contained only general charges, the truth of which would be difficult to prove, yet which reflected on the governor's good name. The first, on February 8, had been suggested by a column in the *Gazette*. It took notice, at least, that Alexander's shafts were beginning to tell.

"Your appearance in print at last gives a pleasure to many. . . . Therefore you had much better . . . come to what the people in this city and province think are the points in question; to wit: They think, as matters now stand, that their lives and properties are precarious, and that slavery is like to be entailed on them and their posterity if some past things be not amended; and this they collect from many past proceedings. . . .

"You gentlemen think, that things past are right, and that things may go on in the same way, without such consequence. . . . You have most reason to fear, that your posterity will be the first to fall, by establishing unbridled power.

"As the liberty of the press is now struck at, which is the safeguard of all our other liberties; this starts another point worth discussing, which by many was thought would never have needed to have been handled here more than it has been. And undoubtedly it is one of the first things that ought to be examined into, fairly and before the world."

A Latin title is prefixed, to please the gentlemen: *Lege fraenata omnis potestas esto;* "Let every power be bridled by the law."

In the same issue Alexander called the roll of the grand jury, who had heroically called the attention of the governor to the lamentable condition of the fortifications of New York; the good Dutch names included Bancker, Boelen, Cuyler, Duane, Goelet, Hammersley, Provoost, Rutgers, Schuyler, and Van Wyck. English names were French, Lynch, Moore, Searle, Richard, and Stevenson.

On April 8, in No. 23, Alexander returned to the attack in an imaginary conversation of some gentlemen upon New York's loss of men and money.

"One that was then moving to Pennsylvania (to which place it is reported several considerable men are removing), expressed in terms very moving, great concern for the circumstances of New York; he seemed to think them very much owing to the influence that some men (he called them tools) had in the administration; said he was now going from them, and was not to be hurt by any measures they should take; but could not help having some concern for the welfare of his countrymen, and should be glad to hear that the assembly would exert themselves as became them, by showing that they have the interest of their country more at heart than the gratification of any private view of any of their members, or being affected by the smiles or frowns of a governor, both which ought equally to be despised when the interest of their country is at stake.

" 'You,' says he, 'complain of the lawyers, but I think the law itself is at an end: we see men's deeds destroyed; judges arbitrarily displaced; new courts created without consent of the legislature, by which it seems to me juries are taken away when a governor pleases; men of known estates denied their votes, contrary to the received practice, the best expositor of any law; who is then in that province that can call anything his own, or enjoy his liberty longer than those in the administration will condescend to let him do it? For which reason I have left it; and I believe more will.' One of the company replied, 'If these are illegal impositions why don't your assembly impeach the authors of them?'

" 'Impeach?' says a gentleman (once an officer of the customs) 'would you have the mob and canaille impeach gentlemen? American assemblies that have only the power to make paltry by-laws, pretend to the power of a British parliament? But besides, should they be mad enough to impeach, that impeachment cannot be tried.'

". . . 'Should they use their authority as they might (said a gentleman), they could make the proudest of you tremble.' "

Little was needed, after such exchanges, to break out into open conflict.

The city election of 1734, taking place on September 30, was the trigger that sparked the explosion. Two saucy songs, whose substance, if not the form, certainly sprang from Alexander's fertile mind, appeared at the victory banquets of the Whigs, and spread the infection of independency. Such boldness, rare in political songs of the day, roused the fury of the Tories. The second song, though pedestrian enough, was set to the tune, "Now, now, you Tories all shall bow."

At the same time three issues of the *Journal*, Nos. 47, 48, and 49, appeared in the very midst of the bitterly fought campaign, beginning September 23.

Public excitement mounted when No. 47 directly charged the governor with the illegal, and what was worse, the act disobedient to his instructions from his lords in England, of sitting and voting in the Council when it sat as a purely legislative body to consider bills passed by the Assembly.

No. 48 charged the governor with a second illegal and disobedient proceeding of adjourning the Assembly when it was not in session, and in his own name, instead of the king's.

No. 49, which broke the restless camel's back, gave in full the resolution of the staunch farmers of Goshen, congratulating Colonel Vincent Matthews for his courageous stand in the legislature against the iniquitous acts of Francis Harrison.

It contained also this rebellious and practically treasonable declaration:

"The authority by which our laws receive their life do not depend upon the will and pleasure of any man, or upon a mere opinion of the judges, who are only instructed to execute the laws; or any other than the plain and positive authority of those who make them."

Observe the total absence of reference to the king's will; for no bill of the Assembly, even when approved by the Council and signed by the governor, could then become law except by sanction *in the king's name* from the Board of Trade and the Privy Council. To omit this phrase in any official message of the governor was a very serious offense, in the eyes of the London bureaucrats. It was beginning to seem a bit stale, to colonial taste, but Alexander hugely enjoyed twitting Cosby for leaving it out. He saw to it that his charges were kept on file at the trade office in London. The board censured Cosby severely for the error, and referred to the public accusation.

Of one notorious violation, charged by the city of Albany, the journalist skated on thin ice. Of the governor, "whom God preserve and make an example of good to all succeeding governors," he said, "I do not know whether Cosby destroyed the deed of Albany lands, but if he did, I do not believe it was done by advice of a lawyer."

Of his agents, cowardice was more than hinted. In the famous No. 7, he had said, "A governor turns rogue, and because it is difficult to obtain relief against him, it is prudent to keep in with him and join in roguery."

This was hitting uncomfortably close. An even stronger hint was given in the September elections, when only one governor's man was elected. Alexander gloated over the victory on October 7. "The virtue and vigor of the inhabitants of this city have been such on this occasion as deserves a better pen than mine to give it its due praise."

Special offense was taken by DeLancey and his friends at the broadcasting of the two songs in the streets, after the Whigs' victory on September 30. Alexander's interest in them—he published poems upon their burning—was so great as to rouse the suspicion that he wrote them. He was no poet.

The last verse of the second song is convivial enough to excuse its lamentable poetry.

> "Come, fill a bumper, fill it up
>   Unto our aldermen!
> For common council! fill the cup,
>   And take it o'er again!
> While they with us resolve to stand,
>   For liberty and law,
> We'll drink their healths with hat in hand;
>   Whorraa! Whorraa! Whorraa!

A song made upon the election of
new magistrates to the city

Tune: "To you, fair ladies now on land"

"To you, good lads, that dare oppose
 All lawless power and might,
You are the theme that we have chose,
 And to your praise we write;
You dared to show your faces brave
In spite of every abject slave,
 With a fa la, la la la, la.

"Your votes you gave for those brave men
 Who boasting aid despise;
And never prostituted pen
 To certify the lies
That were drawn up to put in chains
As well our nymphs as happy swains,
 With a fa la, la la la, la.

"And tho' the great men frown at this,
 What need have you to care?
Still let them fret and talk amiss,
 You'll show you boldly dare
Stand up to save your country dear,
In spite of usquebaugh and beer.
 With a fa la, la la la, la.

"They begged and prayed for one year more,
 But it was all in vain
No wolawants you'd have, you swore;
 By Jove, you made it plain!
So sent them home to take their rest, —
And here's a health unto the best!
 With a fa la, la la la, la."

DeLancey scornfully disposed of the "ribald" songs as the product of heavy, half-witted men. Evidently they hit home. They
were printed on a broadside, and sung, no doubt, at a banquet in
honor of the election of Alexander's friends to the common Council
of the city.

Governor Cosby had injected himself into the campaign; his
entertainments had been prodigious feasts of roasted oxen and the
vol-au-vents of the ballad. Alexander showed special pique at the
feasts provided by "Jerry the Agent" (Dunbar) at Perth Amboy—
of course at Chandos' expense.

It was these insignificant songs that triggered the explosion; the arrest and trial of John Peter Zenger, the victory at law for free speech and press, and the first amendment to the Constitution—the early steps can be easily traced.

Not till the songs appeared, and men were humming them about the streets, did Justice DeLancey take action. He brought them with the offensive papers before the grand jury. Ordinarily a perfectly restrained young man, he lost his temper when someone asked why such things should be called libels. "If these are not libellous," he shouted, "then I am a perjured man."

The grand jury refused to indict. Francis Harrison then decided to make his bid for fame. He was a desperate man, with lawsuits hanging over him. He would precipitate matters, and perhaps escape in the melée he had caused. In the word of Shakespeare's Pistol, he would "infamonize" Alexander by burning the papers, as the House of Commons, in 1710, had burned the sermons of the Reverend Dr. Henry Sacheverell, a noted Jacobite of the time.

Provided with authority from the governor and Council, Harrison first attended the Assembly. They laid the matter on the table. He sought out the mayor, Council, and alderman. One and all the victorious party did not see their way clear to attend the *auto da fé*.

He went to the city court. They put him on the spot. Whence had he the precedent for this atrocious act. He muttered, "Sacheverell." The court asked, did he think himself the House of Commons, then? He departed, muttering. They were just going to add, that if he had read a little more in history, he would have learned that burning Sacheverell's sermons caused the downfall of the Whig ministry. Did he wish a like fate?

The sulky buffoon kept on to the sheriff. The hangman, who was designated as the official incinerator, was diplomatically absent. A domestic servant of the sheriff, with Francis Harrison and "Jerry the Agent"—Chandos' private eye—as the sole witnesses, burned the songs and the offending papers 7, 47, 48, 49, upon the Bowling Green, on the second of November.

The *Journal* came boldly out with the charge of the denial of free speech. Two days after the bonfire, the *Journal* defiantly said, "We may write what we please; but then we must take care, that what pleases us pleases our masters too. We may write; but if we do not write as they think fit, they'll make us smart for it! O glorious liberty! *O rara felicitas temporum!*"

Alexander's use of Latin was no mere pretension. In the offending No. 48 he had borrowed from Horace a sentiment (*Odes*, III, xxiv, 35-36), *"Quid leges sine moribus vanae proficiunt?"* ("What good are mere laws without principle?")

In January, 1735, the offending issues were laid before the New York Assembly and were "found not proper to be burnt" (No. 63).

In No. 64 Alexander asked, "What makes a patriot?" He answered, a patriot is one who promotes the welfare of his commonwealth as his simple duty and as a principle of honor, loving his friends but showing no prejudice against his enemies; above all, a man of courage and firmness, fighting for liberty of speech and freedom of press but showing impartiality, allowing others the same rights he demands.

The very foundations of society were sinking. The Cosby party could not delay. DeLancey gave his nod; the attorney general Richard Bradley, swore out a warrant for Zenger's arrest on "information," a form of indictment when a regular warrant is not "available." The printer was taken into custody on November 17, and remained in prison more than eight months.

The impossible bail of £800 was set; although his friends offered their bond for him, it was refused. Alexander argued strenuously against such excessive bail. The principle became the basis of the eighth article of the Bill of Rights.

On the week before Zenger's arrest, Alexander boldly published "Cato" on libels. Presaging the injury to the printer and his press, he set up the motto *virescit vulnere virtus* (courage thrives on wounds).

The stouthearted Palatine, aided by his faithful wife and his kind friends, never faltered. In No. 63 (January 13, 1735) "Snyder," a Palatine from camp (Germantown, Albany County), wrote a letter to Zenger, rejoicing that the people had refused to allow chips from their shops to be used for the bonfire.

Why was he arrested on the Lord's Day?

Why had he been denied an early trial?

How long must he linger in jail?

"I hope that though you are a poor Palatine, you have still good German blood in your veins."

On July 16, 1735, two weeks before the trial of Zenger, Governor Cosby held a parade and display of the new battery, for which the present Battery Park is named. An ox was roasted whole, and the new cannon were fired in the governor's honor. As the last linstock was applied to the touchhole, the untested piece of ordnance blew up with a great crash. Sheriff John H. Symes and lovely Catherine Courtlandt, only daughter of Philip Van Courtlandt of Cosby's Council, were killed.

Some counted this for a very bad omen against the governor's policy, in that the partisan and the innocent alike suffered. But superstition was never rampant among the Dutch. One more black mark was chalked up against the governor's neglect to drill his gunners properly. The *Journal*, which described the scene, made no capital out of the tragedy.

Alexander cherished a more generous idea. He had discovered the power of a free press, and he revelled on it. He determined, as he put it, to rivet the people's minds upon the one thing—that Cosby must go, because he was deeply and irretrievably unjust. The great journalist's articles in Zenger's paper, his *Letters on Free Speech* in Franklin's paper, his broadsides, vindications, complaints and opinions; his bills in chancery to come, his fight to print the names of the voters in assembly divisions, the publication of their minutes; his dissents at council meetings; his publishing of Indian treaties, of all land sales and surveys; his petitions to the Lords of Trade and his reports to the same body; all had but one idea—that public events must never be kept private.

He was, if any man can be said to be, the first surveyor, recorder, and advocate of the Fourth Estate. And the laborer in the harvest— he operated his own bindery. At the vendue of Governor Burnet's effects in 1729 the young scribbler bought nothing but blank paper —hundreds of reams, for which he paid thirty-six pounds.

CHAPTER VIII

The briefing of Andrew Hamilton

AT THE MOMENT OF John Peter Zenger's trial, the fortunes of his friend and patron were almost desperate. He had been threatened with assassination, and was, in the opinion of his circle, in danger when he walked the streets. His letters had been opened by the venal postmaster. The governor and his friends pleaded with the ministry to transport him to England to be tried for sedition and rebellion. His friends remained with him as a group, but did not come out openly as individuals. Some of them helped him with articles for his *Journal,* but their indiscretions alarmed his more cautious supporters, some of whom, like Kennedy and Colden, took cover and even countenanced the opposition when the crisis was past. Only Rip Van Dam stood with him and shared the enemies' malice.

He had one strong support—the rising public clamor for the truth, which he had carefully nursed into outburst in his *Journal.* If he could reach this support, through the medium of twelve good men and true, he might yet win. Only one case could reach the jury, that of John Peter Zenger; and this only if he could stir the ambitious and hot-tempered DeLancey to bring it about. Cosby and Clarke kept everything else in chancery; but DeLancey had his eye upon the public voice as well as Alexander. He knew that there was at the time a widespread fear of the tyranny of Star Chamber cancery.

At the justice's hearing on the case of John Peter Zenger, Alexander and Smith declined to recognize the jurisdiction of the Supreme Court of the province, upon the ground that the commissions for the judges had never been submitted to the king's Council for their advice and consent.

With the jury lay the advocate's last defense. A jury had twice convicted Harrison, his fellow councillor, in spite of the most prominent attorneys for the defense. The city election had gone for his friends and against the governor. He knew that he could not keep up a delaying campaign much longer. Morris was in England, and had met no early success. The suit against the Oblong had been filed at last.

If Alexander could win a verdict for Zenger, the winds of popular opinion would ride to hurricane force. They might sweep away the other suits.

To concentrate opinion upon it, something must be done to heighten indignation. The people of New York did not care much about poor Palatines, of whom there lived only a handful. Most of them lived upriver, or had gone to Pennsylvania.

Alexander knew how much DeLancey was bent upon punishing Zenger. Meeting him one day on the street, he had treated the printer outrageously. If he could raise that warmth against himself, with a heavy fine or even a short sentence on contempt of court, it would be Alexander—and Smith, too, perhaps, on whom attention would center. Then, indeed, he would have reason to feel that he might win. It was worth the risk. Such reasoning seems a fair inference from the events of the day, and from Alexander's intense probe of every possible escape from a hopeless situation.

The quixotic element in his makeup no doubt set him forward upon the risk. Whatever punishment was in store for Zenger, he alone stood responsible. William Smith he knew to be as stubborn as he, upon principle. But though he had done well on a point of law for Van Dam, he could scarcely have the skill to outwit DeLancey. Though he had assembled an unassailable array of facts proving the truth of the accusations in the *Journal,* they constituted a libel, unless proved true, even in his own book. Alexander had dwelt so long upon the nature of libel in his *Journal* articles, that he knew DeLancey would be ready to meet the challenge, even if he had to silence the pleader. Smith he might control, but an attorney from abroad might have a better chance.

In his first attempt to direct the grand jury to consider the libels in the *Journal,* in January of 1734 DeLancey had told the jury quite correctly that the judge had the duty to declare a statement libelous.

On this Alexander said in the *Remarks* he printed as a commentary:

"I have always thought it the proper attitude of a jury, and not of a judge, to determine what papers were libellous.

"His Honor's intimate acquaintance with the governor, no doubt makes him capable to judge what effect libelling or anything else will have upon his temper; but what condition a man is in when under the government of a temper unsuitable to pass laws for the public good, I won't presume to ask his Honor, because I take the question to be more suitable for a physician.

"Libels are to be published, but every writing disagreeable to a magistrate is not by his construction to be wrought up into a libel against the government; if it is, the liberty of men will not long survive the liberty of the press."

Here was the gist of Alexander's case. The chief justice asserted the libels, because he had seen the effect they had had upon the governor, rendering him incapable to govern. But was Cosby really fit to govern at any time? If not, let us leave the poor man to his doctor.

Alexander in fact knew the *Journal* articles were libelous; but were they libels? Not if proved true, and declared in behalf of the people.

Whether moved by these or other considerations, the two attorneys took their dangerous step forward. The chief justice was not prepared for so bold a move. He told them to consider very carefully what they did, lest the consequences be most unwelcome. They answered that they had fully considered the matter. They maintained their exception to the jurisdiction of the judges' commissions.

Next morning the chief justice summoned the two attorneys. Smith asked to be heard in his own defense. He wished to show that it was always the right of a subject at the bar to be permitted to deny the judge's commission if he deemed it wrong. DeLancey replied that he would neither permit Smith to argue his defense, nor to be heard upon the plea. William Smith said he was so satisfied with the right of the subject to offer the exception that "he durst venture his life upon it."

Justice DeLancey silenced him, knowing of Smith's popularity as a public orator. "You thought you would have gained a great deal of applause and popularity, as you did in the court of exchequer; but you have brought it to this point, that either we must go from the bench, or you from the bar; therefore, you must go from the bar."

"No good arguments certainly," commented Dr. Colden upon the pleas, "but rather that the judge himself thought them unanswerable." Alexander tried to point out the difference between their exceptions and those which they had made against the court of exchequer, which Cosby had erected. In the latter case, he contended that no such court had ever been established by law in the colony; in the Zenger case the exceptions were to the commissions to the judges, not to the court as such. DeLancey shrugged off this point. He would hear nothing more upon the matter.

John Chambers, a respectable attorney, was designated defense counsel in their place, and the trial was set for the fourth of August. John Peter Zenger lay in jail some nine months. His devoted wife aroused public pity as his substitute. During all this time, his family were supplied with food and the newspaper continued by Alexander and his friends.

The next abuse of power was a sordid one. Jurors in those days were "struck" from the roll of freeholders. The first forty-eight names not yet called were put on a new list. Each side then in turn "struck out" the name of the man considered most obnoxious. This was continued until twelve names only remained. This became the jury.

In Zenger's case the original list was tampered with, and was found packed with Cosby's supporters. DeLancey, to whom Chambers complained, ordered a true list. At the last moment, the clerk of the court substituted another list of twelve for those struck. This also was detected and DeLancey, who at least did not rest his power on such chicanery, ordered the true list to be taken. These good men and true earned their record:

Hermanus Rutgers	Edward Mann
Stanley Holmes	John Bell
Samuel Weaver	Egbert Van Borsen
Andrew Marschalk	Thomas Hunt
Benjamin Hildreth	Abraham Kateltas
John Goelet	Hercules Wendover

The numerous attendance at the courthouse on the day of the trial was almost entirely composed of Alexander's friends, as the issue proved. The *Journal* had been careful to recruit them in letters to the editor. Zenger's fellow Palatines lived on Staten Island, on the Newburgh tract owned by Alexander and Colden, and far up the Hudson on Livingston land. The respectable yeomen of Ridgefield in Connecticut and Goshen in Orange County, had most reason to support Alexander. He had secured the liberty of their townsman, William Truesdell, and the Orange militia colonel, Vincent Matthews. The Quakers of Perth Amboy and Eastchester were equally indebted to him for his defense of their right to vote. Robert Lurting, the mayor of New York, and his common Council, who had scorned the governor's command to attend the burning of the *Journal*, would not have missed the fun. Their election to office had produced the two scandalous songs which were part of the ground of libel. As attorney for the Dutch church and the Jewish merchants, Alexander's removal had excited the widest sympathy of a large section of the city. It was little wonder that Dr. Colden could not see how any reasonable man would precipitate such an issue, under such conditions.

At the moment when counsel for the defense was called upon, Alexander sprang his great surprise. He had persuaded his friend and fellow Scot, Andrew Hamilton, famous in Philadelphia for learning and sagacity, to share with Chambers the defense of John Peter Zenger. Alexander wrote the invitation to Hamilton, and circulated it among his friends, with a subscription list. Lewis Morris, Jr., subscribed, but refused to be the only subscriber. Philip Livingston also subscribed, but hoped that a majority of the Council would join Alexander in the invitation. Smith refused to sign; whether he subscribed is doubtful. He called the trial a farce.

Andrew Hamilton had come to Philadelphia and risen to be speaker of the Assembly. He was a great admirer of the Quaker province, and appears never to have taken sides in any issue of importance against its governor. His reputation was high in New Jersey also, where he had accepted a retainer and a grant of 375 acres of land from the Proprietors. Neither as legislator nor as a barrister did he distinguish himself in political controversy as an outstanding Whig. His popularity lay in his legal ability as counsel, and in his conciliating temperament. Alexander gave him his greatest hour of fame, and he rose superbly to the occasion.

Hamilton was fifty-nine years of age. He had won his fame by his personal integrity, his soundness in law, and above all by his stirring oratory. He is perhaps best known to history as the man who built the beautiful Court House, which is now called "Independence Hall." Such a man was beyond detraction. His great prestige was undoubtedly the cause of DeLancey's singular weakness in ruling his opinions, and especially in his summing up to the jury.

According to family tradition, Alexander entrusted his papers to his wife, who sewed them in her voluminous petticoats, and left by sloop for Perth Amboy, thence by chaise to Philadelphia, where she delivered them to Hamilton. Nothing is more likely. Alexander could not trust the mails; he could not leave New York, being a marked man. Hamilton at the trial merely said that he had been able to look over the papers, and was then familiar with them.

The brief for the defense was Alexander's work. In the Rutherfurd Collection, in his own handwriting, it was preserved—a brochure of thirty folio pages. Hamilton referred to it in his argument, and mailed his own copy, as nearly as he could recollect, to be used by Alexander with full editorial freedom, in his *Brief Narrative* under Zenger's name. Thus at every stage in his own cautionary strategy the people's advocate managed the entire affair.

Alexander's narrative dramatically sets forth Hamilton's astonishing skill in seeming to give up his case and then to redeem it. He accepted on behalf of Zenger the fact of the printer's responsibility for the things he had printed. Richard Bradley, the governor's attorney, was thunderstruck; in his mind, this was the whole case. There was nothing further to be done but to request the chief justice to sentence the prisoner. "Not so fast," said Andrew Hamilton, "the jury must still decide whether the facts as stated actually constituted a criminal libel." This, he contended, was just as much a fact as was the printer's ink upon the printed page.

Judge DeLancey ruled against Hamilton on his pleas. His contentions may be summarized as follows:

1. Only the judge may rule whether the statement complained of is a libel.
2. The jury may render their verdict only as to the fact that the libel took place in a certain print at a certain time, etc.
3. The truth or falsity of the libel is of no importance in law. If true, the libel is the worse for it.
4. The defendant may not offer to prove the truth of the libel, nor the honesty of the defendant, nor the public standing of the complainant, in extenuation.

Although the judge had forbidden him to speak on any of these matters, Hamilton had used his great skill in debate to affirm the illegality of all four. Hamilton's pleas, according to Mr. M. Gatley, an English authority of the Inner Temple, are the law today in England and America. Thus the whole argument of Andrew Hamilton, which the judge threw out of court when Hamilton offered to prove the truth of the statements complained of, is under our present laws the essential requirement of the defendant's case.

1. A judge may *not* decide whether a statement is a libel. He may only define the nature of a libel.
2. Only the *jury* may decide whether a certain statement is libelous.
3. The *falsity* of a libel is assumed in a complaint, and accepted as such in the charge by the law.
4. The defendant, to secure a verdict of not guilty, must prove the *truth* of the statement, his *honesty* in making it, and the *public nature* of the plaintiff's position.

Hamilton thus addressed the jury:

"You are citizens of New York. You are really what the law assumes you to be, honest and lawful men, and according to my brief, the facts which we offer to prove were not committed in a corner. They are notoriously known to be true. Therefore in your justice lies our safety."

Five minutes later, he thus returned to the charge:

"When a ruler of a people brings his personal failings, but much more his vices, into his administration, and the people find themselves affected by them either in their liberties or properties, that will alter the case mightily; and all the things that are said in favor of rulers and of dignitaries and upon the side of power, will not be able to stop people's mouths when they feel themselves oppressed." The attorney interrupting, Hamilton hastily added, "I mean in a free government."

The angry attorney interjected, "Pray, Mr. Hamilton, have a care what you say. I don't like these liberties."

But Hamilton kept right on, skirting the periphery of the very subject forbidden.

"It is true that men in power are harder to be come at for wrongs they do either to a private person or to the public, especially a governor in the plantations, where they insist upon an exemption from any complaints," etc. . . .

Again,

"When they come to know that a chief magistrate abuses the power with which he is trusted for the good of the people," etc. . . .

"A governor who has places (I will not say pensions, for I believe they seldom give that to another which they can keep to themselves) to bestow can keep the same assembly for near twice seven years together.

"We all very well understand the true reason why gentlemen take such great pains and make such great interest to be appointed governors," etc. . . .

"But will anyone say that all or any of these good ends are to be effected by a governor's setting his people together by the ears," etc. . . .

Thus, although never referring to Governor Cosby by name or specific, Hamilton managed to draw his portrait in vitriolic strokes. No wonder Peter Collinson, the Quaker merchant of London, and Alexander's friend in trade, wrote to him after reading his *Brief Narrative:* "How could the governor bear to see his portrait sketched so boldly before all the people?"

In his peroration, the great attorney placed the Zenger cause in its proper setting:

"The question before the court and you, gentlemen of the jury, is not of small or private concern. It is not the cause of one poor man, nor of New York alone, which you are trying. No! it may in its consequence affect every free man that lives under a British government on the main of America. It is the best cause. It is the cause of liberty. And I make no doubt but your upright conduct this day will not only entitle you to the love and respect of your fellow citizens, but every man who prefers freedom to a life of slavery, will bless and honor you as men who have baffled the attempt of tyranny, and by an impartial and uncorrupt verdict have laid a noble foundation for securing to ourselves, our posterity, and our neighbors, that to which nature and the laws of our country have given us a right—the liberty of both exposing and opposing arbitrary power (in these parts of the world at least) by speaking and writing truth."

The jury withdrew, and after a very little while, brought in their verdict, "Not guilty." Upon the pronouncing it, the numerous audience expressed their joy in three loud huzzas. Scarcely one person except the officers of the court were observed not to join in this noisy acclamation.

The shouting crowd poured out into the streets; the houses were soon decorated; the battery fired a salute, which was echoed by the guns of the station ship in the harbor, with a grand banquet following.

Dr. Colden reflected upon the event that,
"one might think after such aversion to the prosecution appeared from all sorts of people that it would have been thought prudent to have desisted from further proceedings, but the violent resentment of many who had been exposed in Zenger's papers together with the advantage they thought of gaining by his papers being found libellous by a jury, blinded their eyes that they did not see what any amount of common understanding would have seen and did see."

In the following month Andrew Hamilton returned to New York to attend a banquet in his honor. A gold watch was presented to him in a gold box, on which were inscribed Latin mottoes:

"The laws were overturned and liberty intimidated. Nevertheless, these things march again. So may it always happen to him who has deserved well of the republic."

Reflecting upon Hamilton's plea, Colden went on to say,

"As to the merits of the case, it seems probable that falsehood in all cases is not necessary to make a libel, but malice is, and falsehood is a sure proof of the malice." [The modern ruling is that the court assumes the falsehood of the alleged libel. It does not have to be proved; what has to be proved is the truth.]
"Andrew Hamilton seems to know it is libel if private faults are exposed of men in power which do not affect the public.
"As to the exposing of faults or crimes in public office, there can be no fault or crime in doing it in a republic, and as the constitution of

England has a considerable share of democracy in its composition, our constitution allows for complaints of this order."

After the trial, Alexander hastened to the printer's office and began the preparation of the *Brief Narrative* from the stenographic notes. He sought the verdict of posterity upon his entire argument.

The substance of the defense which he had prepared for Andrew Hamilton to use, but which had been ruled out by the chief justice, was used by him in reply to an attack upon the plea published in the *Barbadoes Gazette* and later reprinted. He sent his reply to Benjamin Franklin, who had followed the case in his *Pennsylvania Gazette,* and it appeared in several "letters" in that newspaper beginning on November 10, 1737. Most of this he also reprinted at the time in the *New York Weekly Journal,* the last letter being somewhat abbreviated for lack of space. His "brief narrative" is available both in Dr. Colden's letters published by the New York Historical Society, and in Vincent Buranelli's admirably "edited" text of 1957. He reprints also a part of the letters. The two documents together constitute the classical eighteenth-century statement upon this fundamental human right.

Not only in the matter of free speech and free press, but arbitrary imprisonment, cruel penalties, excessive bail, ignorance of the nature of an indictment of a prisoner, and indeed the whole due process of law, were all incorporated in Alexander's courageous defense against the corrupt and arbitrary administration of Governor William Cosby and his associates.

Alexander's style is definitely modern, though it recites the ancient precedence in deference to his audience. How modern it is can only be realized if one reads similar pleas of contemporary attorneys. It may well be compared with the brilliant oratory of Andrew Hamilton, who took Alexander's brief and infused it with excellence.

When the Constitution was adopted, the authors of the original text were under the impression that the state constitutions, all of which contained a Bill of Rights, were a sufficient protection. The public, however, thought otherwise and the omission almost caused the defeat of the Constitution. The chief contender for the inclusion of the Bill of Rights in the Federal Constitution was Governor George Clinton of the State of New York, who had carried a chain in the surveys which his father made for James Alexander.

It remained for another pupil of Alexander to summarize public opinion by quoting from one of England's dramatists. William Livingston, satirist and gadfly of the Revolution, quoted in his *Independent Reflector* in 1752 from *The Fawn* of John Marston:

> "Freeness, so 't grow not to licentiousness,
> Is grateful to just states. Most spotless kingdom,
> And men, O happy! born under good stars,
> Where what is honest, you may freely think,
> Speak what you think, and write what you do speak,
> Not bound to servile soothings."

Alexander's *Brief Narrative of the Case and Trial of John Peter Zenger* won its ultimate victory, not in the courts of a colonial empire, but in American minds and hearts. No legal precedent had been created. Libel remained libel, no matter how true, no matter how necessary to be spoken for the common weal.

The victory, for victory it was, lay with a jury who had defied the law, and acquitted a poor printer. They had agreed with Alexander who had said in the *Journal* "Laws are not always the measure of right and wrong." They affirmed with him: "the exposure of public wickedness can never be a libel, in the very nature of things."

Whatever that means, there is no denying that the *Brief Narrative* is a triumph of American journalism, the classic appearance of a new art. Writing in Zenger's own person, Alexander became America's first ghost writer. In a sense, the book is fiction, although honestly documentary. It is irresistibly absorbing. It carries the reader along, however ignorant of law he may be, until he becomes completely involved in a dramatization of an American courtroom. Think how it must have swept along the readers of 1735.

For good and all, the reader enlists in Zenger's cause. Who cares whether the verdict of freedom of the press was the law then or a century later? The verdict was more than legal; it was right.

CHAPTER IX

Something of a constitution

AFTER THE HAPPY conclusion of the trial of Peter Zenger, the court and the country settled back into an uneasy truce. The city took up its daily round again. The leaders had no rest.

Alexander immediately announced the publication of the narrative of Zenger's trial. He urged Andrew Hamilton to send his notes and asked for authority to publish. Hamilton complied with a letter to "Dear Jim." He sent his copy to the advocate with full authority to alter as he pleased.

The *Narrative,* with Zenger as author, appeared in a few weeks. An immediate republication followed in legal circles, which did not end for a century. In England the action of the courageous jury engaged a vast interest in liberal circles. The famous defender of libel cases, Lord Erskine, had the honor of a dedication of one edition. Charles James Fox carried a measure through Commons in 1792 incorporating the principle of lawfulness for truth in defense of liberty.

In the colonies Alexander's precedent prevailed only under liberal patronage. Censorship by government was clamped down in New York. William Livingston's journals were suppressed for less than Alexander had printed. The Assembly on one occasion at least hauled printers before them and forced apologies and recantations. Not until the Stamp Act resistance in 1765 did men print freely again.

For the moment, however, the *Journal* continued its course, though without renewed attacks. Alexander and Smith petitioned the Assembly to restore them to the bar. Their address was an eloquent justification of their course.

James DeLancey, however, had come to the conclusion that his way to power in the future would lead through the political authority of a chief justice rather than his legal acumen. He was, *ex officio,* a member of the governor's Council. His numerous kindred, widely distributed over the great estates of New York, were already powerful in the Assembly. He could weld them into a solid block of reaction, making him the power behind the governor.

Thus he became the first great boss of political New York, using every device exploited in after years by his successors. Corruption and intimidation were the arts by which he beat his way to dominance. The only man who refused to bend the knee was James Alexander.

Controlling both governor and Assembly from the bench of the chief justice, DeLancey was able to immobilize New York's part in the French wars, and to continue the Albany-Montreal commerce.

Yet, for all that, he remained the courteous gentleman, the promoter of church and college, the patron of science. With Alexander, who matched him in professional detachment, he remained on terms of courteous intercourse, and even in cooperation on cultural projects. Alexander's granddaughter married his grandnephew, while Colden, who suffered most from his political hate, became reconciled to his son's marriage with DeLancey's niece.

The digression is necessary for an understanding of the background of James Alexander's later career. Scorning the political demoralization of his opponent's methods, and rigidly loyal to his own sense of honor, he became a good-natured Coriolanus, declining to ask for office, though ardently desirous of all. As DeLancey forsook law while running a political machine from the bench, Alexander used his legal and official connections to maintain his political ideas. The careers of the two men invite a more acute study as pioneers in two of the great American arts of government.

Judges DeLancey and Philipse attended the Assembly at which Alexander presented his plea for reinstatement. Though required to withdraw before the vote was taken, it was on Philipse's motion that a negative action was taken.

Governor Cosby died in March, 1736, under circumstances that led to surmises of intrigue of an Oriental kind, in which Senior Councillor Clarke and Judge DeLancey figured as rivals, Clarke, who had managed the Cosby deals in Mohawk lands, won the race. He succeeded in promulgating a decree of the dying man, suspending Van Dam from Council and thus leaving Clarke as deputy governor on Cosby's death.

Alexander and Van Dam entered their dissent, and confusion followed with two claimants officiating. Clarke dissolved the Assembly, and in the September vote Alexander, Smith, and young Morris were triumphantly elected. Colonel Morris returned from

England with news of the confirmation of Governor Clarke. The Lords had found Cosby's grounds insufficient to warrant his dismissal of the chief justice, but not wrong enough to provide a reinstatement. DeLancey's London connections were too strong for that.

Alexander had joined New Jersey Whigs at this time in petitioning a separate governor for the province. Morris assumed the chair, and the Lords confirmed it, glad to be out of the discord.

With the advocate now the leader of a hostile Assembly DeLancey no longer opposed his reinstatement to the bar. With Colden and Murray as mediators the minute was erased from the chief justice's record, and the two attorneys returned to practise the law, without more words. DeLancey thus avoided an expensive suit for damages, and possible action by the Lords Justices of England, a branch of the parliamentary structure that was incorruptible.

In the fall of 1735 Alexander's supporters had won a municipal election. The advocate had supported them vigorously in the campaign and praised the mayor and his board for the things they had *not* done. These included gifts to their own members, spending their time at city expense, serving alien powers, stopping work on the theft of the city's great seal, flattering the powerful, using market money for other purposes.

They had printed the charter of the city (which Alexander had helped to write); they had asked the Assembly to supply a police force, and, when refused, they had supplied it; they had built and filled a workhouse.

His one regret was that they had refused Alexander's request that they address the governor to urge Harrison's dismissal as recorder. But, he went on, "Mr. Harrison has now fled the city, and another has been appointed . . . I forgive them." Alexander's agreement not to seek further recompense was a generous act and a characteristic one.

His term in the Assembly was an *annus mirabilis,* a two-year period of utopian hopes. His hopes of what might be accomplished had already been expressed in Zenger's *Journal,* in the form of "A Recipe for Distemper in the Body Politic."

"Let the body move constantly, with good store of reasons, four drams of caution, with a handful of prudence wrapt in the leaves of magna carta. Apply these to the head upon any monstrous protuberance, and in one week's time the herb magna carta will dissipate all protuberances and render the body easy. If there happen any oppression upon the vital parts, let the root of free election be applied immediately and frequently to the whole body, at least once every three years. But as it is a root that soon putrifies, there must be great art in the gathering of it."

Alexander knew, of course, that laws without principle were empty verbiage. Something more constructive was needed. He set it forth as part of an essay on liberty.

"To secure well that foundation, liberty, the way we have not far to seek. 'Tis but looking to the constitution of our mother country, copying after it as near as circumstances will admit.

"We see there the mere process of government, all in perfection, each independent of the other, and balancing and checking the other two parts: the king to execute the laws and preserve the peace; the council of the best men of the province; the last part, with free and frequent elections of the assembly, the democratic part, to make the laws as the representatives of the people."

So far as can be learned, this is the earliest use of the phrase "checking and balancing," as applied to the machinery of government. It is an American phrase. England, with all ultimate power in the House of Commons, had no use for it.

Ten years later Alexander wrote the fragment quoted above, which he kept in his own notes, unfinished. Apparently it is a comment upon his plan of the division of powers and a system of checks and balances which he was the first to devise. Colden supported Alexander's opinion that without such checks no power of the government, whether executive, legislative, or consultative, could be fully trusted. Integrity, he thought, must be the first quality demanded of councillors, but he was not even sure that this would always be obtained. Experience seemed to show the opposite.

Neither Colden nor Alexander seemed to have set down on paper any specific plan at this time for constitutional measures of control. They apparently trusted to the courage and patriotism of members of each power to maintain their own rights, and restrain the excesses of others.

In turning to the Country party the governor consulted Alexander; finding him in this optimistic mood, he suggested he would be glad to approve the adoption of laws which would serve as a foundation for Alexander's constitution. The advocate described the negotiations in his letter:

"[after the election] his greatest former opposers were chosen—amongst which I happen to be one—he promised to give some good laws to give us something of a constitution (besides will and pleasure) in consideration of which we granted him full salary and all his arrears—not at all in affection. I believe he owes it much to me that he got it . . . [voted] from year to year."

Alexander's use of the phrase "will and pleasure" was incautious. It was words like these that led Clarke to complain that Alexander was treading very near to treason. "The King's will and pleasure" comprised all the positive acts of the English Government, of Parliament, and its councils and committees; all those acts of grace by which the English Government continued men in office, approved the actions of officials, or indulged a province in some overstepping of its prerogative. It was obviously Alexander's intention to create on the American shore a constitution modeled upon that in England, but not dependent upon it.

Four years of arbitrary misrule had taught Alexander the advantages of a more representative government. His aim in planning "beyond will and pleasure" was directed toward the transfer of still further powers to the colonial legislature. Governor Clarke's willingness to cooperate with him gave him the incentive to undertake an extensive reform. The comprehensive measures his party proposed in the session of 1737 suggest months of careful study and discussion by the members of the Assembly.

Its power rested with Alexander and his two friends from Westchester County. Col. Lewis Morris and his junior son had fought Cosby long and bravely, but neither man was noted for discretion.

The members of the Assembly approached Alexander on the speakership, but the advocate preferred to lead from the floor. Colonel Morris was therefore elected. Alexander accepted the chairmanship of the influential committee on rules and elections. The delegates of Westchester and New York City were chosen to act as a committee to draft the traditional *Reply to the Address from the Governor*. Thus Lewis Morris and Alexander had full liberty to present their idea of a constitution.

The bills proposed in the house and the reforms demanded in the *Reply*, are so numerous that they may be grouped for convenience, without further reference to their place.

Of elections: these must be carried out under set rules, honestly conducted, under the Assembly's control. Dishonest pranks, such as Governor Cosby's packing the Board of Sheriffs with his own men, were severely condemned.

Elections were to be full, free, and frequent. "Full" evidently meant that all various elective offices should be chosen at a single date. "Free" evidently meant a considerable extension of the franchise, how far not indicated. "Frequent" meant at least once in three years. On the merits of the last rule Alexander wrote and published a considerable tract.

Members were forbidden to receive gifts or other emolument. In view of the fact that Alexander still claimed his right to his seat in Council, while holding his Assembly seat, his enemies took advantage of a certain loss of popularity in his case by making a motion to expel him. It was defeated, but the Assembly passed a vote making mandatory what Alexander had promised he would do—withdraw upon restoration to Council. The affair undoubtedly cost him some prestige.

Alexander insisted upon the dignity of the Assembly as he did of all public offices. When the Council in a moment of nonchalance dispatched a mere clerk with a message announcing the Council's actions, Alexander severely condemned the slip, and obtained a vote of censure by the lower house upon the higher. He had in mind, of course, the sanctity of the electoral prerogative, and King Charles I's unhappy fate in its violation.

He listed a series of laws which the governor had no choice but to approve. These concerned the organization of the house into committees, the duties of its members, and its rules of order.

The governor, though invested with respect, was to be just as subject to law as anyone. He might not plead in the king's name, to commit illegality. The real meaning of "that sacred name, the King," was fully explained, its prerogatives limited. Checks must be provided to prevent the abuse of power.

Section 14 of the *Reply* contained the famous message of defiance to Governor Clarke. The Assembly refused to accede to his request for a salary on a permanent basis. The Assembly went farther, making each annual grant conditional upon satisfactory performance of his duties. Thus, in effect, the governor would become a mere creature of the lower house.

It is evident that this part of the reply was the work of Col. Lewis Morris. It was certainly at odds with Alexander's demand for a governor's prerogative in executing the laws. The paragraph ends with a characteristic flourish, "by the grace of God, we propose, etc." Morris was fond of such expletives. Alexander never used one, so far as I have observed. The rest of the document, it is safe to say, was Alexander's. The long preambles, rehearsing precedents of other days, the insistence upon order and good style, on checks and balances, are all of the advocate's making.

The regulation of fees, the reduction of the commissioners on Indian affairs to proper treatment of their Indian guests, with the reduction of their expenses, were all due to him.

From him, too, came the ingenious suggestion that the sales taxes on the purchase of slaves be much increased, and the entire proceeds devoted to promoting the immigration of indentured persons for service.

Alexander was not in the Assembly when that body, now reduced to ignominy, congratulated the governor upon the awful slaughter of the Negro victims of the courts in 1741.

Assembly control of the establishment of future courts was insisted upon. No new offices were to be established except by law of the Assembly.

Most of this was, indeed, "beyond will and pleasure," "something of a constitution," and more. But it was destined to its inevitable annulment by the Privy Council, as an encroachment on the king's prerogative. Alexander, anxious to secure the governor's assent to the laws, and contending that Clarke had been a good governor in his daily routine of office, favored a salary of £1,560, more than double the previous actions. The Assembly approved the sum, but reduced Alexander's five-year term to one year.

Clarke, having obtained his "raise," promptly dissolved the Assembly in October, 1738, thus automatically vetoing all the Assembly actions without recourse, except the budget.

Lewis Morris had fallen ill, and resigned in September, to take up his Jersey appointment. Alexander was suffering from an early appearance of gout. Without their leaders, discouraged by the end of all their utopian schemes, the reformers fell a prey to the determined and well-provided assault of DeLancey, Clarke, Philipse, and the Albany clique. Not a single one of the Alexander team was elected from New York.

Cheating was charged at the polls, which in New York were in the questionable power of Sheriff William Cosby, Jr. Alexander, as usual, made no effort whatever to obtain votes. His honor forbade, but scarcely his common sense.

Yet the battle was not wholly lost. The reforms were published. The minutes of the Assembly were preserved in print. William Smith, Jr., the historian, read them in Alexander's library and described the votes in his widely read history. Clarke could dissolve the Assembly at will; he could not dissolve Alexander's idea. For the first time an American jurist in a royal colony had affirmed the right of self-government. The trail he blazed was one that others could easily follow. It might someday lead to a complete instrument of dominion autonomy.

Such a design was entirely foreign to the English mind. Dr. Colden once commented upon its propensity to adopt shortsighted expedients, instead of deep-laid principles of government.

Yet in their charters and their "instructions" they had themselves created the very instruments they refused to make for themselves. Alexander's contribution to this sort of constitutionalism consisted in the idea that such planning must be based on original experience. New York wanted its own structure of law. The seeds of an American constitution had been sown in a Crown colony.

It is now a commonplace of American thought, that its national character was forged on the frontier. But it has been overlooked that its first frontier was not the wilderness, but the Atlantic Ocean. The inexorable factors of space and time wrought their will upon the European loyalties, and provided their own measures of defense.

When James Alexander realized that a couple of Scotch brooks like the Esk and the Tweed had been traded for three thousand miles of water, he built his independence out of them. Their wide-crested foam, and not the pathless forest, was the firm foundation of his constitution.

The practice was already general throughout the colonies. The "charter colonies" of New England made bastions out of their royal grants. Alexander, with no such safe deposit as a "Royal Oak," built his constitution on ideas, and defended them at law, pamphlet and brief, or legislative enactment.

He had observed that although the New York Charter of Liberties and Privileges had been at once annulled by the Duke of York, the good Dutch had gone ahead as if it was still valid. So when his own law reforms were annulled two years later, or his restraint on the slave trade washed out, he left the mischievous ideas to work freely in minds like the heirs of his thought, William Livingston and John Jay.

He had no authority for his claim that a colony could appropriate what it pleased of British common law, leaving the rest of it at the dock. He merely acted upon it; judges and juries sustained him. The English ministry "indulged" him, for lack of a better idea.

In such a fertile soil the seeds of union and liberty grew better than in Boston violence or the fiery rhetoric of a Patrick Henry.

It was not Henry, but Virginia's Madison, Princeton-trained, who with his New York friends Hamilton and Jay defended the Federal idea, while New York's George Clinton, borrowing the pseudonym of Alexander's oft-quoted *Cato*, fought just as steadfastly to put the Bill of Rights into their constitution.

Alexander, with his engineer's principles of tolerance and balanced drives, had shown the way to get a constitution that would work. When governors had tried to overawe him with mere authority, Alexander did not disdain to raise what he called "the public clamor." The governors had then prudently retired behind the bayonets of Fort George, while the sons of liberty roamed the streets.

The American's general practice of passive resistance consisted in evasion, nullification, or at the worst, removal into the wilderness. There the disaffected might live as he pleased, sometimes in a congregation under the fear of God, sometimes like the lonely proud conquistador of the Catskills, Don Gonzales. But for himself Alexander chose the battle on the eastern frontier, wrestling in the dark of time and distance with the best minds of England. There alone, he thought, would one learn what to do, with freedom as his teacher.

For a quarter-century after 1730, New York had the repute of being the most disturbed of the British provinces. The ferment of ideas worked to the same end in Tory and in Whig. It would increase until William Pitt could truthfully say that New York had drunk most deeply of the baneful cup of infatuation.

Thus Alexander's labors led the way to a new epoch of political thought, which realized his dream of "something of a constitution beyond will and pleasure."

The way, he knew, would be long and full of pitfalls. Meanwhile, there was his law business, now greater than ever because men trusted him. He had spent his money freely in defense of free speech. He must rebuild his fortune, sell his lands and leases, open mines, increase his exports abroad, live as a citizen should, who had a marriageable family.

He wanted money—who did not? His espousal of liberty was based on economic as well as political laws. Trade and manufacture, he contended, flourished only where freedom was the air they breathed.

"What is it that makes trade and manufacture flourish in England and Holland lately, more than in any other part of the world? It's because their liberties are better established and preserved. Trade and manufacture are such dames, that it's only liberty can court and win them to stay with a people, and as soon as liberty departs they fly away, and settle again where liberty does."

The words were written for his paper a quarter of a century before Adam Smith launched upon the same inquiry into the wealth of nations.

CHAPTER X

Leisure of a citizen

Mrs. MARY ALEXANDER was one of the most remarkable of the Scots-Dutch housewives of her day. Her eleventh child Susanna was an infant. She was managing her large store where the sale of a hundred pounds' worth of goods in a morning was no uncommon event. She imported and exported with the West Indies and London. She had a great circle of friends.

To divert her husband from his deep concern over his political failures, she suggested that they should build a new house and make of it the center of a new life. It was the best possible therapy for a man of Alexander's temperament. On Broad Street just north of Wall stood the house of her great-uncle Abraham DePeyster. It was around the corner from the courthouse where Alexander practiced in the Supreme Court. Its gardens stretched down toward the East River as far as the Jews' Alley, where Alexander's good friends and neighbors carried on, with his aid and counsel, the extensive commerce. Though burned in the great fire of Revolutionary days, a description of Alexander's home survives in the account of a granddaughter.

She listed the great and small dining rooms, the great tapestry room on the upper story, the pink damask, red, blue, and green parlors, the reception room, the offices, the many bedrooms. With its large garden with huge box hedges, the rows of "laylocks" and other flowering shrubs, the vegetable garden, and a remarkable "pharmacy" garden of medicinal herbs attractively laid out, it seemed larger than it was in fact.

One may be certain that it was the favorite place of the Dutch lady and her budding daughters. The fact that all three of the older girls married young readers of the law may indicate that the great jurist was not too stern a teacher.

The fourth daughter Joanna and her baby sister Susanna grew up in its shade, where the skyscrapers tower today.

There, if the tradition be true, Mrs. Alexander suggested the formation of a new public library to absorb and enlarge the municipal library which Alexander had helped to start. The historian of the New York Society Library states that the organization took place in Alexander's house on Broad Street, then the center of every enterprise for the public welfare. The formal beginning, following an informal meeting of young friends, was in May, 1754, when James Alexander; his son; his partner's son William Smith; and his three young Livingston associates: Robert R., William, and Philip, organized under the lieutenant governor as a legal board.

Alexander's gratitude to his devoted wife was shown in the entire confidence with which he provided for her in his will of 1745, in which the youngest child's share is given to the mother, and her full guardianship confirmed, to exercise her discretion on the inheritance.

In 1732, and again in 1737, Alexander and Smith had been instrumental in obtaining from the Assembly funds for the salary of a teacher of a new Latin High School, as it was called. The school was to be both free and public. It was to teach "Latin, Greek and all the mathematics," including the engineering studies apparently, of surveying, navigation, and accounting, in all of which James was so proficient.

This, the first free public secular school in New York, was to be limited to twenty youths selected because of their intellectual promise, from New York City and the other counties, on a proportional basis. Once chosen, they could not be dismissed by the schoolmaster, "except for delinquency," presumably failure in studies or disobedience to public law. A Scotsman, Alexander Malcolm, was the schoolmaster. His stipend, at first limited to the surplus "after expenses" of income from pedlars' licenses, later became a part of the regular Assembly budget.

The Latin High School realized Alexander's dream of a regular supply of well-educated leaders, who after their training in law, would assume the responsible posts of government. Though intellectually aristocratic, the selection from all the counties of the province provided at least a democratic representation. Their immunity from dismissal marks the first step toward academic freedom in American educational history.

The school was doubtless an outgrowth of Alexander's contact with the wretched collegiate education which Alexander found among the young clerks who came to read law with him, in preparation for admission to the bar. Most famous, and most unruly, of Alexander's pupils was William Livingston, who with his brother Peter read law from 1744 to 1746. Then in his early twenties, a graduate of Yale, William was a very lively lad about town, though he denied it.

"As to my being abroad almost every night, I have for this month stayed at Mr. Alexander's till 8 and 9 o'clock at night, and shall continue to do so all winter, he instructing us in the mathematics, which is indeed going abroad."

The reference is to the use of the telescope and "circumferenter," a predecessor of the modern surveyor's theodolite. Alexander had been to great trouble in securing one from England. Peter Collinson, his Quaker correspondent, had secured it; George Graham, deputy royal astronomer, had approved it, after observations with it.

In 1745, while profiting by his law studies, Livingston wrote an essay on the apprentice system in law. He hated its drudgery, being entirely without his teacher's tireless thirst for employment.

A second essay of his, also printed in the *Weekly Post Boy*, brought a severe reprimand from his teacher, who taxed him with its authorship. Reprimanded for its "free and offensive tone" (the mild criticism of his biographer), Livingston left Alexander to study under William Smith two years more. The two men soon made up, for Alexander could never hold resentment.

With William Livingston studied William Alexander, James's only son, a bright and ambitious lad. William helped his mother in the store in addition to his studies in mathematics, especially engineering, surveying, and mining. James destined him to be his successor as surveyor general for the Proprietors. On the father's death in 1756 the board immediately complied, though William was embarking for England for a prolonged stay.

Three of Alexander's daughters presently married pupils of the law course. Peter Livingston became William's business partner. John Stevens of Castle Point and Elisha Parker III of Perth Amboy became his partners in legal affairs of the Jerseys. Elisha, who was attorney under James for the East Jersey Proprietors, tells of his own experience.

After the day's employment, he repaired to Mr. Alexander's library, where he summarized his reading for the day; the jurist commented upon it until dinnertime. After dinner Mr. Alexander read from law books himself, commenting as he read, while Elisha took his notes. After a thorough tutorial of this kind through the months, he would be tested, as John Tabor Kempe was tested in the next decade. Theodore Sedgwick has printed from an Alexandrian manuscript the jurist's critique of the young lawyer's presentation apparently at a moot court. It is an excellent job, quite serviceable as a model for a law school of the present time.

In 1743, being concerned lest he die without adequately trained successors, Alexander had obtained permission from the Board of Proprietors of East New Jersey to train young Elisha in the art of surveying. "Whereas, Mr. Alexander is now old," the resolution began. He was then fifty-two. Parker was already reading law with him. He repaid Alexander by marrying his daughter Catherine, and aiding him on the board, as its assistant solicitor, until 1751.

It was as a private citizen that James Alexander stood forth as an advocate of religious liberty. In the case of Rev. Louis Rou against his church trustees for breach of contract, already mentioned, Alexander had contended, like Roger Williams before him, that a clergyman was a citizen, with full rights at common law, not an ecclesiastical court.

As attorney for the Presbytery and for the Reformed Classis of New York, Alexander enabled them to defend their right to hold their property against official and private assault. He gave a church site and a hundred acres of land for a church at his Blue Hill mine in New Jersey. Although not an Episcopalian, he bought half-a-pew right in Trinity Church, New York, to help out his opponent, the Reverend Vesey, in rebuilding the church.

With the cooperation of his colleague, William Livingston, he entered a hearty dissent to Governor DeLancey's attempt to establish King's College on an exclusive basis under the Church of England. With registration open to students of all faiths, with a gesture of tolerance in the appointment of a few trustees not of the English church; and with the establishment of a professor of the Reformed faith as well as the Anglican, he was content to compromise, and accepted election as a trustee. The extended controversy, continued after his death, resulted in the founding of Rutgers, Princeton, and New York Universities.

He was amused by a jeremiad of Parson Taylor, his bitter opponent in Newark, and sent a copy of his tirade against the New Jersey Proprietors to Thomas Penn of Philadelphia, for his entertainment.

But "Lawyer Alexander" as the Dutch churchgoers called him, was essentially secular in his public views, standing for religious liberty as an absolute right, with other rights. No pamphlet religious wars troubled the peace of the Dutch colonies. When the Reverend Frelinghuysen of Albany protested against theatrical performances by the young ladies of his parish, he was asked to resign.

To occupy himself in moments of enforced idleness, Alexander sought science once more. An engineer by training and temperament, he took up with the fashionable post-Newtonian astronomy, making a census of the number of telescopes in the province, (less than a half dozen, it appeared). He corresponded with the astronomer-royal Edmund Halley, on ways of improving his own and other instruments and apparatus.

Alexander's accomplishments in astronomy were more than the polite bowing acquaintance of the English intellectual of the day. Dr. Colden dedicated the pamphlet to him in 1748 which was an introduction to his physical philosophy. In a note to Alexander, Professor J. Betts of Oxford commented upon it, and expressed his thanks for the observations which Alexander had forwarded through Peter Collinson. They concerned the comet of 1748; Dr. Betts, in gratitude for being supplied observations which he had been unable to make owing to atmospheric conditions, added, "The Royal Society and myself are greatly obliged to you." He especially approved Alexander's new method of determining the orbit of the comet.

With Colden the lawyer was in constant touch, following the doctor's speculations on Newton with some doubt. But as he lived in New York, he helped his friend in the publication of his manuscripts, reading and correcting them with great care. Colden wrote him that there was no one else in the province whom he could trust to see his mathematical treatises through the provincial printing press of James Parker.

Through these ties Benjamin Franklin was slowly and insensibly drawn into the Alexandran circle. He had followed the Zenger trial with interest, and in 1737 had printed Alexander's *Letter on Freedom of Speech and Press.*

He had been for some time in correspondence with Colden and Alexander on scientific matters, and had probably seen Colden's proposal for an institute of science in New York, made in 1729. It resembled in some ways the British Royal Society, though it was more in the nature of a club. There were simply not enough men to do more, even in Philadelphia.

Franklin hit upon the same idea of an American Philosophical Society, using the term in its medieval sense of science, natural philosophy (physics), mental philosophy (psychology), and moral philosophy (ethics).

He invited Alexander to be the first member in New York, and to add to the number. Alexander took up the idea with enthusiasm. In a few days he had the signatures of all the principal attorneys in town, as he wrote Colden. The latter was of course an original member. Membership in New York, however, meant little. Alexander took pride in the membership, but there was no comparison at the time between New York and the two older centers, Boston and Philadelphia.

But the miscellany of proceedings, first proposed by Colden nearly twenty years before, he never started. The New Yorker was by far the most learned man in the province, but he was also interested in too many sciences and professions (medicine, law, government, physics, astronomy, botany, and so on) ever to achieve eminence in any. He was also involved in real estate, and more than all else, in politics.

Alexander had made the acquaintance of the great inventor-scientist through the medium of Franklin's *Pennsylvania Gazette*. With Colden and with Archibald Kennedy, the only other New Yorkers who established their taste for political and scientific speculation, they formed a circle which Franklin found it convenient to cultivate. Franklin's apprentice and later successor, James Parker, succeeded Zenger in New York as the publisher of the more liberal newspapers, and added to them a Hartford periodical.

Through his brother, Elisha Parker, young James became an active member of the Board of Proprietors, joining Alexander's group in the great struggle for the perpetuation of its charter.

Thus, out of his defeat with its great drain upon his physical and mental resources, Alexander was enabled to reconstruct a successful life in the city. He had matured his legal philosophy in the thorough education which he gave to his law pupils. His practice at the bar had widened his acquaintance with the citizens of New York and his influence with them. Through his leisure studies in astronomy, he had gradually broadened his acquaintance in other provinces. A great career was still open to him upon a far wider field.

CHAPTER XI

Saving a small province

THE BOARD OF PROPRIETORS of East New Jersey must be one of the oldest business corporations in this country. Their history has been continuous from their original charter in 1683 to the present time. Charles M. Andrews, the great authority on colonial affairs, calls it unique in history, "a notable achievement."

Three volumes of their minutes have been published, the last volume devoted to Alexander's period. The editor says of his work:

"Most illustrious member of the board was James Alexander, to whom credit must be given for the creation of the methods and systems relating to the severance of title, and the drafting of instructions to surveyors of the East and West divisions.

Alexander was in fact America's first great corporation lawyer, a pioneer in the history of American business. The board's minutes show him to be the real executive of the board until his death. Its structure resembled in many ways the modern mutual investment fund. Its expenses were met by quitrents on sales. Subscribers bought shares, or, as their value increased, fractions of shares, thus becoming members of the society. Alexander as early as 1725 voted four and one-half shares, either as owner or as proxy for others like Charles Dunster of Scotland, who wrote him in high praise of his trusteeship.

This mutual land fund company, if it may so be called, issued dividends, not of stock like the mutual fund of today, but of land. The first dividend was, I suppose, the largest, amounting to 10,000 acres of "good right," and 3,000 of "pine right." (*Right* here has its modern business meaning, property per share.)

The dividends were issued in installments about ten years apart.

There were fourteen in the first 150 years (1685-1850). The average dividend of one full share was about 5,000 acres.

At first the Proprietors were confined to Great Britain. Fortunately some of the Proprietors, such as Lord Neill Campbell, uncle of the first Duke of Argyll, and Gawen Lawrie, served as deputy governors of New Jersey, and saw the value of an American directorate on the spot. This was the salvation of the British company, which would otherwise have closed up like so many of the early colonial land schemes and other speculations overseas.

The quitrent, corresponding to the management fee of the mutual fund company, was a device of "immemorial antiquity." In its origin it was a fee paid as quittance for personal service of the manor tenant to his lord. Mortgages with high rates were common, but the quitrent impaired the title to land in fee simple. It was thus unsuited to the American scene; but that was not Alexander's fault. To him it was the business air he breathed.

The Connecticut settlers derived their claim from Governor Nicoll, James II's deputy, who had, without authority, offered land to New Englanders at the time of conquest, in 1664. Alexander derived the board's proprietorship from the duke's grants of charters to his two friends and creditors, Carteret and Berkeley, and their heirs and assigns, the first boards dating in 1683. Between the duke and the Proprietors various purchasers had bought and sold, among them William Penn, whose example in the founding of Pennsylvania at this time greatly influenced New Jersey.

The western division, in particular, filled soon with Germans and Pennsylvania Quakers, who "little respected" their secular lords. In the eastern division, Amboy was laid out by the board, whose Quaker members, such as Lawrie, issued broadsides and pamphlets advertising the beauty of the site, and the incredible richness of Jersey soil, with an enthusiasm that brought several shiploads of colonists before 1690.

These all paid quitrents, to which they were well used. But the earlier settlers refused. Between them the Dutch colonists, who antedated both these groups, had a hard choice; but most of them, being "quiet" people, as Alexander called them, accepted the Proprietors.

This was not the only "error," again to use an Alexandrian word. The board itself had been very careless at times. George Keith had been a good surveyor in past years, but much of the time they were ill served. Gross errors (in one case Alexander mentions an item of 175,000 acres) were made. All of these, he wrote, had been remedied and the leaks stopped, except in one instance.

The deeper Alexander probed into the errors of the past and

their consequences for the present and the future of the land company, the more dissatisfied he became with the measures of alleviation which he had undertaken. They did not go to the root of the matter.

Alexander had been aware of this ever since his reorganization of the American Proprietors in 1726. In 1735 he had written John Hamilton, President of the Proprietors, urging him to call a meeting to stop the steady encroachment by the associated citizens of Elizabethtown.

Ironically enough the conflagration that spread over the quiet acres of New Jersey was fired by a Quaker, John Penn, William Penn's unhappy grandson. Although Franklin despised the poor fellow, he did not detest him as he did his uncle, Thomas Penn. Franklin's long crusade against the Penn family as the political overlords of Pennsylvania, whose word was law, and whose properties were above the right of the Assembly to tax them, ended at last in triumph, but not until 1790, and after a considerable cash settlement.

Alexander, whose contact with the heirs preceded Franklin's by a decade, could congratulate himself that the Jersey Proprietors had surrendered their sovereignty over the government of New Jersey, thus avoiding the greatest error of all the British rule: uniting the ownership of land with feudal overlordship.

In 1740 when John Penn insisted that Alexander should bring suits of eviction against some of Penn's tenants in the Jerseys, Alexander undertook the thankless task. He began the suits in Elizabeth and called in Joseph Murray as his partner. In his *Daybook* for 1740, he recorded that he had found Penn "a very uneasy man of business." Even to himself, he would not set down the consternation he must have experienced. Franklin with less provocation, seldom mentioned the Penns without contempt, which he transmitted even into his documents.

But the word "uneasy" exposed all the most objectionable traits that annoyed the eighteenth-century gentleman. It meant troublesome, disagreeable, unfriendly, on bad terms, dissatisfied, rigid, and uncompromising. All of these meanings were prevalent and well understood by Alexander's associates.

Yet John Penn was a Proprietor of New Jersey with great holdings in the province. As the executive agent of the board, Alexander could not refuse the task. He realized that with proprietary bias on one side and settlers determined to maintain their squatter rights upon the other, the Proprietors must clear their own record and go to the root of the matter. Too many mistakes still clung like barnacles to the economic ship of state.

Considering these and many other "errors," Alexander proposed to the board a complete overhaul, or "perusal," of its records. This was approved. Alexander started his reading in October, 1740, and completed it in June, 1742, a task of eighteen months, of the most intense study and classifying of all the deeds.

He was now prepared to present the Proprietors' claims in the whole eastern division. Retaining all the lawyers who would accept his fee, he went ahead with the preparation of a bill in chancery, against one Benjamin Bond and others, who had refused to pay their quitrents.

Associating Joseph Murray, David Ogden, and Robert Kinsey as aids, more perhaps to prevent their accepting retainers from the other side than because he needed them, he set about the final reading, which he completed in 1743.

For two years more he worked on details of printing. The original bill filled eighteen skins, each 24 inches by 27 inches, beautifully written, with great columns of figures and names, a veritable encyclopedia of the province. The brief in itself constituted a complete history of the settlement of New Jersey, and is a source-book today.

Not until 1746 did Alexander read proof. The volume of large folio contained eighty-one pages with schedules of nearly as much again. Twenty-seven pages were taken up with description of Newark riots. There were also the speech of Alexander's friend, Judge Samuel Neville, to the House of Assembly, May, 1746, and two articles from a newspaper.

The maps were made by Lewis Evans of Philadelphia, through Benjamin Franklin. The latter was paid £1 15 s. 1 d. for his services in contacting Evans.

Franklin later offered to engrave the maps, and his offer was accepted. The maps were hand-colored; George Duykinck, an artist, was contacted for this. Whether he did the work is not known. In all, the book cost about £300 for 250 copies, making it perhaps the costliest printing exercise of the time. In effect it won the case without a trial.

The kernel of resistance, on the basis of patents from Governor Nicolls was Monmouth County, stretched around to Sandy Hook. Here, too, was the last resistance to the Alexander campaign of settlement by due process of law. The hard core of the resistance never gave in, however, either in Monmouth or nearby in Elizabeth.

It was Alexander's achievement, that he contained the mischief within this narrow shore line, and uprooted the spread of the weed from the rest of the province.

In his reply to the Newark defense, Alexander admitted three cases of error. One has been mentioned; the sellers were in that instance compelled to make restitution. In another case, the "Ramopoch" patent, some 50,000 acres were given away by deeds from an unauthorized surveyor, through the dictate of a corrupt governor, Cornbury, in a grant to his secretary, Pierre Fauconnier. In his old age Fauconnier was represented by his daughter Mme. Valleau, whose daughter Suzanne became the wife of the celebrated physician, Dr. John Bard.

After long suits, and some riots, the Valleau claims were compromised and the board's authority established. Alexander purchased her father's "ninth" in the Nine Partners lot in Dutchess County, New York.

There originated the famous secret society of the Clinker Lot Right Men, mentioned by Alexander as the head and front of the insurrection. A certain dividend of land in Elizabeth, known as the Clinker Lot (Dutch *klinker,* brick), was used to distribute "rights" to those who could be trusted with the secrets of the society. Arising some time before 1740, it was one of the first manifestations in the history of protest in the colonies. It would be imitated in Albany County, New York, after 1750, under the sponsorship of Massachusetts land-jumpers. It would be repeated in 1766 in Dutchess County, New York, under the like sponsorship of Connecticut men.

Alexander dated the commencement of violence at September 15, 1745, when Samuel Baldwin was "peaceably" released by the Newark chapter. The rioters were so considerate as to repair the jail door which they had broken open. Others were less thoughtful.

Jonathan Hampton, a surveyor, wrote Alexander that Governor Belcher had brought from Boston a set of canting Puritan preachers to Essex County, who shouted their provocations on every street corner.

Alexander's own armed tenants prevented any use of force, but a thousand pounds of damage was done. Alexander, however, brought no suit. He claimed that throughout the occupancy of the Proprietors there had been no breach of peace with the Indians, no Indian had been maltreated, and no Indian deeds were claimed on the Horse Neck patent.

A Scot, Dalrymple, no doubt kin to the Master of Stair, who was chairman of the British Proprietors, was turned out in the bitter winter cold with his wife, long pregnant, and the children. On the first occasion pity was heeded; on the second, a complete job was done. A parson was identified in the attackers.

The death of Governor Morris in 1746 produced a short moratorium. The country was at war with France. In the absence of an appointed governor, John Hamilton took office as president of the Council. He was a sick man, however, and died soon. Alexander was the real head of state. Laying aside the hostility to the Assembly, he worked cordially with his opponents to create a Jersey regiment for the expedition against Canada. The quota of five hundred men was more than filled.

As time passed, Robert Hunter Morris sailed for London to represent the Council's interests. The young man did his best to help his friend. In 1751 the Lords of Trade sent a sharp letter to the governor, demanding that the riots should cease, and hinting broadly of the probability that a commission to investigate would soon be on the way to Perth Amboy. Morris pleased the Penns and was made governor of Pennsylvania.

Governor Belcher, who had thought himself securely fixed in office through influential friends, went into a tailspin of fear and panic. He realized that if his active connivance with the settlers were made known, he would be in a dangerous spot, and he turned about full circle. Richard Partridge, the agent in London for the Assembly and governor, was Belcher's own brother-in-law. Under the nepotic rules of the day, Belcher would at once be held responsible for Partridge's every move.

"Interest yourself no further in the rioters," he wrote. "Be careful! Be careful! Anything you may do will be the ruin of me and my family." The rioters were a vile company of miscreants. He would have no more to do with them.

One of Alexander's last acts was to wait on Governor Belcher with a petition from the Council to the king, against the violence in New York's attitude. "Tell me what to do, and I will do it," Belcher said very humbly.

He arranged in 1747 for "an act of grace." Any rioter who stopped rioting and obeyed the laws would receive a pardon. This was repudiated by the Lords of Trade in 1751. Few took advantage of it at once, but Judge Neville in Newark noted that the attitude of many rioters seemed to be softening.

In November, 1749, a great riot occurred at Horse Neck. Abraham Phillips, a complier, was robbed; his roof was pulled off his house. Men now carried guns; a large number were shot off in the streets, to the great fright of citizens. This seemed going too far.

Alexander now sent two large "chronicles of the disorders and outrages" to the Lords of Trade. The governor in December, 1750, issued simultaneous proclamations in Essex on the Atlantic side, and Hunterdon on the Delaware, ordering an end to the rioting.

In April, 1752, he protested strongly against a jailbreak in Perth Amboy. Alexander, who had employed one Boyle to ride to every riot and collect depositions while irons were hot, noticed that the same small group of provocators traveled from place to place inciting the disorders. It was no longer a popular uprising, but a mob.

At last, in 1755, came the sign of surrender. The settlers announced that they were ready to treat. Alexander replied that he was ready. Judge Neville held court in Essex County where sixty rioters came in, "confessed indictment, were fined in small sums by the court, and bound over to good behavior for three years, with costs."

"By the appearance of the rioters," Alexander wrote, "I have reason to believe the spirit of rioting is very much eased in the county of Essex." Some, he believed, had a real dislike to the crime, others feared His Majesty's forces now arriving to join Braddock's army would be brought against them, in case they persisted in resisting the legal authority.

"Essex people," wrote David Ogden, "are generally sensible of their errors in the many riots committed."

The end was in sight, but Alexander was not satisfied. He persuaded John Stevens, his strong and courageous son-in-law, to tour the whole province with Ogden, talking with individual rioters, persuading them of the justice of the Proprietors' cause, and offering free pardons and generous leases. His own leases permitted a tenant to enter on the land, paying nothing for the first three years, then signing a "fair and equitable lease" by mutual agreement, or buying out in fee if able. Such a lease, after her husband's death, was offered by Mrs. Alexander to one Terwilliger, as "Mr. Alexander's practice."

Stevens kept in close touch with his father-in-law as he traveled about, enthusiastically reporting that hundreds of men were turning to accept his terms. He found only that in Elizabeth, though most signed, a considerable group remained intransigent.

Ogden at this time suggested a dummy suit in the court which would impress the unregenerate. Even though a mere dumb show, many would be frightened by it.

Alexander, the victor by legal means alone, would have none of it.

"It smacks too much of the other side," he wrote. "I would not do it, not though all Jersey joined."

A new threat had risen to overshadow the internal strife. It centered in New York, where Alexander had been recalled. "I am much a stranger to affairs in New York," he wrote to his friend in 1750. Colden, who grew querulous with advancing years, suggested that he would do well to keep out of them as a private citizen of the province. James returned a soft answer.

Later in the year Halifax yielded to Governor Clinton's pleadings and restored Alexander to his rightful seat in New York's Council. Clinton, however, was allowed to plead his poor health, and returned to London in 1753.

DeLancey, once in the seat of power as lieutenant governor, lost no time in thwarting Alexander's hopes of establishing his survey line on the Jersey border. At the suggestion of his agent in London, DeLancey appealed to the Privy Council, which in 1752 handed down a decision annulling not merely Alexander's survey, but the whole original agreement in Hunter's time. Hunter's authority even to make the survey was denied, because he had not asked the Lords of Trade to run it.

Young Mr. William Pitt was one of the signers to the Lords' report. It brought dismay to New Jersey, triumph to New York, tumult and confusion along the Delaware valley.

The beautiful Delaware River rises in two parallel branches that spring from the western Catskills. The west branch makes a three-quarter turn at the town of Deposit, and becomes for a few miles the northeastern bound of Pennsylvania. At Hancock the east branch, which up till now has been on a parallel course, hits the western sister head on. From Calicoon, past Cochecton, where Alexander had fixed New Jersey's northern point, the new river turns south to Narrowsburg till it reaches Minisink Ford. There it turns east by south eighteen miles to Port Jervis, the present Jersey boundary point, once called Mahakamak, swirling past Pond Eddy. The names are significant of the unruly river.

Ever since James Alexander's first venture in surveying, this region had been disturbed by clashes between New York and New Jersey. Governor Burnet had sternly reprimanded the quarreling settlers, and had for a dozen years brought comparative quiet. Then the troubles began again.

By 1740, twenty years and more after the fixing of the Alexandric line, the troubles had increased. They could no longer be ignored. The Jersey line ran uncomfortably close to Goshen, the county seat. Led by a tough Dutchman named Swartwout, and supported by Sheriff Thomas DeKey, a colonel of militia, the Yorkers made their strife official. Behind them stood Chief Justice James DeLancey, whose control of the legislature depended upon his support of local causes. He also owned major shares in the great patents on the border.

From the fixed point on the Delaware River at Cochecton Eddy, some twenty odd miles above Port Jervis, depended not only the New York boundary southeastward, but another boundary line hung in a southerly direction as far as Little Egg Harbor on the coast of Jersey. This divided the proprieties of Eastern from Western Jersey, no longer a political line—though counties used it as a local bound—but essential to the orderly business of the two great proprietary land companies of East and West. In that affair Alexander, as surveyor general of both companies, was very deeply concerned.

In 1743, failing to get any consent from New York, Alexander persuaded Governor Morris to consent to the running of his proprietary line. John Lawrence, his son's friend and brother-in-law to be, put the line through. In spite of much opposition both at the time and in later years, this line has remained the division line of the two great proprietary companies, the boundary of several counties, and a line defining the widening gap in social and financial ways, between the two Jerseys. To most people, even the residents of the state, "the Jerseys" is a term of unknown meaning.

It seemed absurd to have a division survey between East and West Jersey, without a corresponding one between New York and New Jersey. In 1748 Alexander obtained a Jersey law authorizing it. New York had persistently refused to cooperate.

Judge DeLancey was then in high favor in Britain, where his brother-in-law, Admiral Peter Warren, was toasted as the hero of Louisburg, captured in that year. The time was propitious for a bold attack on New Jersey. Robert Charles was appointed agent of New York interests in London.

He presented an appeal for a committee to review the Jersey line. William Pitt, Grenville, Oswald, and Horatio Walpole were appointed. They recommended the annulment of the whole division line, as Robert Hunter had never received official sanction from the ministry. The line, in effect, was as if it had never been drawn. All that remained was the formality of approval by the board and the Privy Council. But the English Proprietors, well forewarned, interposed an objection and request to be heard; Alexander, for the American Proprietors, began immediately the compilation of one of his famous bills in dissent, running to some forty articles. Even DeLancey was moved to call it a "rather remarkable report," but not to characterize it more specifically.

He was rather moved to impugn Alexander's character and position by calling him and his friends "a most virulent and active faction of Presbyterians and Free Thinkers."

James Alexander and Samuel Neville were chosen a committee

to defend the settlers' rights. He at once sent word to Colonel Van Camp to prepare his regiment.

Robert Charles, even before the public announcement of the decision of 1753, sent the chief justice his thoughts on the matter. It had been the claim of the New York opponents of the act of 1748 that the words 41° 40′ in the agreement were merely affirmative words, in the legal sense; merely descriptive aids, and not definitive, as the phrase "northernmost branch of the Delaware" was acknowledged to be.

But what was the northernmost branch? Obviously, the river itself; thus the head of Delaware Bay should be the real point of division. In that case New York touched Philadelphia.

Or, if that seems too drastic, the Forks of Delaware, the "Water Gap" area; Easton, where the large Lehigh River joins the Delaware. This Pennsylvania site exactly west of New York, is obviously the place intended by Governor Dongan, standout for the Forks of Delaware, our "natural" line of division.

DeLancey was a lazy and easygoing fellow, but once roused, capable of great force. He was still only chief justice. Clinton was about to leave, however, and a new governor, Sir Danvers Osborn, was expected. The nephew of Lord Halifax, his goodwill was essential. He could wait to entrap him.

Osborn's sudden death upon arrival set DeLancey free to move. In March, 1754, he obtained a vote from the New York Legislature, and in May he wrote Governor Belcher that he intended to take the whole northern section of New Jersey into New York, inclusive from the eastern New York boundary. "The Forks of Delaware are the ne plus ultra of New Jersey," he wrote; a fine phrase, indeed. In the same month Alexander sent the memorial of the Proprietors to the Board of Trade, with his batch of depositions regarding riots and dispersions on the division line.

DeLancey, rather nonchalantly, also informed the Lords of Trade of his letter to Governor Belcher. It was a bold and arrogant step, but it was not arrogant enough. Had it been followed up by action, it had a chance of success, for England was now at one of the lowest points in its parliamentary history. Henry Pelham, the prime minister, had died, and the Duke of Newcastle, his brother, had great difficulty in keeping any sort of government together.

The governor decided for strategic reasons to accept Alexander's offer to refer the dispute to a commission to be appointed by His Majesty. He had served on such a commission, that for settlement of the Rhode Island line; he knew how many things could happen in such bodies. He knew Pitt was on his side.

But in the meantime he secured from the Council of New York the authority to exercise the jurisdiction of the disputed district up to the Easton–New York line. "Which," he wrote to the governor of New Jersey, "accordingly, I do."

Alexander and his friend Kennedy entered their dissents to the motion. It was routine for Alexander; for Kennedy it was an act of great courage, for he was conservative through and through. But his wife's properties lay in the Jerseys.

DeLancey issued a proclamation, calling upon the people of upper Jersey to come under his benign rule until the act was settled by the king. Alexander, of course, issued his own proclamation against it. He also ordered Colonel Van Camp to resist all attempts at sovereignty over New Jersey. He went himself to the border to observe.

Governor DeLancey left the fighting to others. His sheriff, Colonel Thomas DeKey of Orange County, took matters into his own hands. Hearing that Alexander had two surveyors in the field, Harvey and Gardner, he crossed into Jersey, assaulted the surveyors, and smashed their equipment. He also sent word to his acquaintance for fifteen miles inside the Jersey line, to come into his regiment. The Jerseymen retaliated by rabbling him and his property in Jersey.

Seeing the Jerseymen inclined to defend themselves, the local leaders came to terms. A committee of John Alsop, William McEvers, and John Morin Scott, met Judge Neville and Alexander. After some impertinent bickering of Scott, which Alexander chose to forget, it was agreed that each side should write identical letters to the public, expressing regret for any breach of the law, and urging the people to remain quiet. Alexander took command of the Jersey militia and ordered its colonel to march his troops to the boundary.

Against such men DeLancey's efforts at corruption would be fruitless. The extent of his intrigues, in the endeavor to discourage New Jersey from resistance to his usurpation of authority, appeared in a new quarter during the spring and summer. Hunterdon County, New Jersey, was then the largest unit in the province, occupying a position similar to that of Albany in New York, as repository of undistributed lands. It covered most of the Delaware River region. Morris County was carved out of its northeastern bounds in 1747. The riots in the following year coincided with New York's appeal against Alexander's move for the New York division line.

Now, with the renewal of the same dispute, the inhabitants met, to the number of several hundred, and petitioned the government of Connecticut to set them off in a separate county of that colony.

According to David Ogden's report, they claimed that they had bought their land, but had been unable to find any evidence that any other persons had any right thereto. There were "sundry depositions, and the signatures of a considerable number of people."

The Council labeled the uprising a conspiracy, and made further investigation. Alexander wrote President Clapp of Yale College, whom he knew to be of great authority and influence throughout the colony, asking him to use his efforts in discouraging the legislature from joining in the conspiracy. Connecticut did, however, extend a welcome to the Hunterdonians.

Ogden reported:

"The color pretended for the conspiracy rises from the uncertainty of the southern and western boundaries of the charter of the colony of Connecticut; and had there been nothing afterwards to ascertain these boundaries yet there was no more color to claim any part of New Jersey by virtue of that charter than there was to claim Mexico, Peru, or Brazil; for New Jersey was at that time in the possession of the Dutch (1662)."

Alexander himself told the Council, that "the past trouble and charge about that line will be but little compared with what is very likely hereafter to happen."

How far DeLancey would have gone is uncertain. He was a headstrong man. But the great majority of New Yorkers had never been interested in the claims; the Jerseys, on the other hand, were ready to fight.

DeLancey may have had some vague idea of a deal with Connecticut, by which under "color" of Hunterdon's annexation the whole of southern Jersey would fall to that colony, while New York absorbed the north. The case of Maine, and that of Vermont, in New England, were certainly no less violent in the appropriation of land by another colony. Dog eat dog was the rule, and would be so, Alexander believed, unless some firm union was established by His Majesty.

On the petition of John Stevens and James Parker, the governor at last, on March 1, 1755, issued a proclamation reinforcing the demand of the Lords of Trade that the great riots should cease. The presence of English regular troops, who arrived to reinforce the regiments already in America, also conveyed a solid hint to the ringleaders, that the heyday of misrule was drawing to a close.

It seemed to Governor Belcher a "curious affair," meaning evidently that he admired its intricacy of plot within plot, but that it was beyond his understanding. Ill with the gout, he could not really govern. The Council, unanimous for Alexander, did his work for him.

Alexander, concerned lest DeLancey's act should intimidate the unsteady rulers at home, wrote to the New Jersey Proprietors' agent, Ferdinand John Paris. Between the lines the bold leadership of Alexander, resolute to resist to the utmost, can be seen.

"On the 17th of December the Council of New York broke silence at last as to the many applications and references to them and made a report of which I immediately demanded a copy from Mr. Banyar, clerk of the Council, but have not obtained it to this day—but I have been more successful with the printer, and have got some copies from him.

"Whether I shall have proper time to make remarks before this ship goes I know not, other than that they agree not to the proposals appearing by the order to Col. Van Camp of November 23d last for the preservation of the peace, and advise vigorous measures for subjecting as much as they can of New Jersey to the jurisdiction of New York—if what's thereby advised be attempted, there will be an actual war upon the borders which when once kindled God only knows the end of it.

"The people of New Jersey near the line are convinced that they have a just cause and many of them will as soon lose their lives as give up their estates to New York, which they are satisfied is the consequence of submitting to the jurisdiction of New York.

"On the other hand . . . the majority of the people of New York near the line believe that the proprietors of Minisink and Wawayanda are in the wrong, and abhor their proceedings and act only by compulsion; and heavily complain of the oppressions they themselves suffer by keeping up a watch of 25 or 30 men at Col. DeKey's house and another watch at Goshen jail; from whence we have reason to suspect the people of New Jersey may make them repent the kindling of the war, if they attempt it—as I believe they will.

"I am now grown old, and by the course of nature will before long be disabled to give the proprietors of East Jersey such assistance in these affairs as I have done for many years past; and when I shall be so, then the care of their affairs (by what I now see) must devolve upon Governor Morris and my son.

"We have talked several times at the council of proprietors that you must be well advanced in years, and of the difficulties they should be under were they deprived of your assistance in their affairs; and especially in this difference with New York; wherefore they would be well pleased you should give a handsome fee to some gentleman you can depend upon, to take the trouble to inform himself of what you know concerning their affairs, to assist you in case of sickness, and to supply yourself in case of other disability; for we see little prospect of a speedy end to this New York dispute, and even if a commission were ordered at equal charge, we are apprehensive that as long as our antagonists can by the assembly have command of the whole purse of the province of New York against us, that all blocks whatever will be laid in the way of a determination, in order finally to weary us out, and by some base composition to prevail on us to give up some part of our rights—which neither I nor any other (I believe) of the proprietors has the least thought of doing, because we are fully satisfied of the justice of intent we insist on; which I believe the other side cannot with a good conscience say."

In September, 1755, came the solution of all the plotting. Sir Charles Hardy, a fighting naval officer, stepped aboard the good ship *New York* and took command. De Lancey's day was done, so far as the New Jersey defense was concerned. The Lords of Trade had annulled DeLancey's act of the previous December 17.

In severe terms, Lord Halifax rebuked the governor's actions in interfering with a case under consideration, and thus prejudging his superiors' verdict.

Alexander's faith had its reward; on June 27, 1755, the New York act of December, 1754, was repealed by the Privy Council, and a commission of impartial judges ordered, chosen by the two provinces, with the addition of king's representatives. Each province was to pay its share of the cost.

James Alexander allowed an expression of satisfaction to escape him. "The act of December last is damned and thrown out of doors," he wrote Colden. But the New Jersey line, he admitted, now teetered precariously on the balance, the Pitt committee's vote of disapproval being still in the works somewhere, and capable of being revived for approval by His Majesty.

He wasted no worry about it, however. Tired out as he was, with an attack of gout approaching, he braced himself for new endeavors.

To conclude the story of the Jersey line, the Alexander team continued his defense for twenty years without their leader. Stevens and Rutherfurd were on the last commission. Charles Clinton's son James made the final survey in 1775. The term "41° 40′ north latitude" had won the day, but was arbitrarily set at Mahakamak. Thus a large part of Minisink went to New York, but by far the greater part of Delaware River remained with the Jerseys. The present line starts from Port Jervis, its "tri-state" point surrounded by a state park whose lake bears the name of Rutherfurd.

CHAPTER XII

The hopes of union

THE IDEA OF UNION—social, philosophical, political—was not a late growth in Alexander's thought, though it was long before it became his ruling passion. In January, 1745, he had taken the initiative in the promotion of a political union of traders, to resist the first aggressive steps by Parliament to destroy what little liberty remained in the colonial structure of government. He had written enthusiastically at the time to Dr. Colden:

"We lately got a copy here of a bill brought into the house of commons last session of Parliament, to prevent all paper bills in the plantation to be issued hereafter from being tenders, and to our great surprise found two clauses foisted in at the end of it, making the instructions of the King or of any by his authority obligatory on governors councils and assemblys in the plantations and all laws orders etc. by them to the contrary to be void, which if passed would subject the plantations to the King's absolute will.

"Never was there so near an union in any place as there was in this against these clauses; a meeting was had of the principal inhabitants without distinction of parties. It was agreed to remit £150 sterling to Messrs Baker's to employ an agent and counsel, and to join with the gentlemen of West India islands and Virginia in opposition to these clauses, before house of commons and house of Lords, and each agreed to write to their correspondents in London to countenance this application to the utmost of their power. The money was immediately raised and remitted for that purpose by Stephen DeLancey and Co. with orders if more be necessary to advance it, with orders also to promote the passing of the bill so far as concerned paper money which was excellently well drawn, and proper to prevent in time the mischiefs arising by paper money being a tender; leaving it still in the power of the government to issue securities for money on an exigency taking care of good funds and to pay the interest to those who will please to accept them. I am

"Yrs

"Jas. Alexander"

On a Sunday in October, 1753, His Majesty's ship *Arundel* dropped anchor in New York harbor. Alexander perhaps wondered whether the ship's name, so familiar to him, had a note of warning in it.

Sir Danvers Osborn, His Majesty's newly appointed governor, was greeted by James DeLancey, who had received from Admiral Clinton the Wednesday preceding his own notice of appointment as lieutenant governor.

The welcome of New York, a proverbially cheerful town, was all that any governor could wish. James DeLancey thought nothing so fine had ever been known.

Unfortunately in a way, Sir Danvers' voyage had been too short and easy. The governor's mansion in the fort had not yet been completely prepared. Mr. Joseph Murray, the councillor, placed his house on the Broadway at Sir Danvers' disposal.

Banquets and other gaieties filled the week; but it was observed that the gallant officer took all his pleasures sadly. Great things were expected of him, too much, perhaps, even though he was the brother-in-law of the Earl of Halifax, the president of the Board of Trade.

On Friday afternoon, he was found tied to a fence post in the Murray garden, "strangled with his own handkerchief."

All men knew how eager DeLancey had been for the governorship. He had even offered to buy it of Admiral Clinton. But none thought him involved in Sir Danvers' unfortunate death. Still, to ease men's minds, the Council requested Mr. DeLancey to appoint a committee to inquire into the death of Sir Danvers Osborn. This special committee consisted of James Alexander, senior councillor present, Judge Chambers of the Supreme Court, and Mayor Holland of New York.

At a committee meeting Mr. Thomas Pownall, Sir Danvers' secretary, was sent for and was asked for his "instructions." He refused to surrender them, unless an order came from the lieutenant governor in Council. This order accordingly was made, and Pownall delivered the documents. He enclosed in his report to the Board of Trade an attested copy of DeLancey's order and the order in Council. The orders in trade he left under seal with Mr. Murray. He pledged himself to tell nothing that he should not. William Livingston reported that only Alexander's skill prevented a real clash between Lieutenant Governor DeLancey and Mr. Pownall. Fearing that at such a critical time trouble might arise, he suggested the compromise. The instructions thus became known.

Two of the instructions excited special notice. The governor was enjoined to reduce the disorderly people of New York to their due obedience. The governor was to call a congress of commissioners, to prepare a plan of union of the colonies, its duties being to secure the Indians more closely to the British interest, and to organize for the defense of His Majesty's dominions.

Among Pownall's new friends in New York were two councillors, Archibald Kennedy and his friend James Alexander. From Kennedy Pownall received valuable aid of statistical nature: population, prosperity, taxes, and a moderate view of the value of America to England. From Alexander the young publicist got much more: an intimate acquaintance with New York affairs. The friendship ripened to warm regard on both sides. Pownall was an enthusiast of intercourse. "When I become a friend, 'tis with the whole heart, believe me," he wrote to Sir William Johnson, who was then acting as referee in a Dutchess County suit at Alexander's request.

In early spring Pownall went to Philadelphia, as the bearer of letters from Alexander to Franklin and Richard Peters, secretary of the colony. Peters wrote James an appreciation of Pownall. He expected that the young man might become of much benefit to the proprietary cause so dear to his own employer, Mr. Thomas Penn, the Proprietor. At present, he said, Mr. Pownall, was occupied with "the theater, electricity, and the Assembly." The good Quaker could not have named in all Philadelphia three things more distasteful to himself. But it is clear that the young man was finding out all he could, from Mr. Franklin and his friends in the popular house, of the shortcomings of proprietary rule in Pennsylvania.

In April Mr. Peters continued his correspondence with William Alexander, the councillor's son. Mr. Franklin and he were coming to the congress at Albany, as commissioners. Mr. Pownall would accompany them. They would spend a night at Amboy, guests of Alexander. They would be most grateful for the furnishing of a sloop to waft them to Albany. The friendship had ripened apace.

Alexander in the following May apprised Dr. Colden of an interview with young Mr. Pownall. The Englishman had been busy on his own account, in preparing a plan of union for the colonies in the coming war. The plan, which he afterward published, was not bad so far as it went.

Pownall contended that the attack by water—by sea, by the

great rivers St. Lawrence and Hudson, and by the great lakes—furnished the quickest and securest way to victory. So, indeed, after many failures, it proved.

He would begin by building one good vessel of draft on Lake Ontario, with a fleet of lesser craft to dispose of canoes and the lesser vessels. Seizing Niagara would at once cut the continental line of French forts and outposts in the Alleghenies.

Alexander must have come to like the young man greatly, to trust him implicitly, and to respect his talents. He told Pownall that Dr. Colden had suggested such a scheme in recent letters, which he had sent on to Franklin and Peters. With further talk, he decided to share with the young traveler the plan that Benjamin Franklin had left with him, as the outcome of a recent stay in New York.

The talk of the three men—Franklin, Peters, and Alexander—had turned upon the necessity of union, and the problem of how to gain an efficient direction of such a union, while at the same time protecting the liberties of the colonies. Evidently it was Alexander who propounded the problem; for Mr. Franklin responded that he had some thoughts on the matter which he would send Alexander.

Accordingly Alexander received them, and after his own perusal he sent them on with his suggestions to Dr. Colden. Colden studied the plans at his leisure, and forwarded the comments to Franklin. Unfortunately, the congress had proceeded at a more rapid pace than his own philosophy; the notes arrived when the debate was almost at an end. Franklin expressed his regrets that he could not use them.

Colden's notes could not have helped the schemers in their draft of a first Plan of Union. His comments were negative. He suspected the authority of the commissioners, the likelihood of approval, the rushing into war without more thought of the Indians.

Alexander's proposal, on the other hand, was concrete and to the point. His letter to Franklin has not survived. Its chief emphasis seems to have been his favorite device of checks and balances. He wrote Colden the gist of it.

"To me it seems extremely well digested, and at first sight, avoids many difficulties that had occurred to me.

"Some difficulties still remain; for example there cannot be found men sufficiently skilled in warlike affairs, to be chosen for the grand council, and there's danger in communicating to them the schemes to be put in execution, for fear of a discovery to the enemy.

"Whether this may not be in some measure remedied by a council of war, of a few persons to be chosen by the grand council at their stated meetings, which council of state to be always attending the captain general, and with him to digest beforehand all matters to be laid before the next grand council.

"The governor general and council of state to issue the orders for payment of monies so far as the grand council have beforehand agreed, to lay transactions before the grand council at every meeting, so much as is safe to be made public.

"This council of state to be something like that of the United Provinces [of the Netherlands] and the Grand Council to resemble the States General.

"The council of state members to be chosen for capabilities only, not representation."

What Alexander called the Council of State was called in Holland the College of Deputed Councillors; a sort of vigilance committee of the united provinces of Holland in continuous session administering the agencies of government, watching over the treasury, and protecting the people's interest against a tyrannical stadholder or a runaway assembly—a supreme court, cabinet, and upper house, all in one efficient body, which had made the Dutch Government the envy of Europe. Napoleon ended it fifty years later.

Each man thus proposed the plan in which he felt most at home. Franklin hated vested interests, though he was himself planning to be a proprietor on a grand scale in the Ohio lands. Alexander put his trust in a smoothly working union of power, brains, and wisely managed capital. Franklin became a publicist; Alexander remained the engineer.

The congress went for Franklin's plan by a unanimous vote, after much discussion. They stated the taxes in general terms, had the grand council elected by assemblies, and kept in provincial authority the collection of the taxes.

The Indians came at the end of the session; their speeches and rewards were purely formal; they made and got no promises. This was of course DeLancey's doing. The Indian nations were thus alienated before the war had started.

Alexander wrote to Colden, to tell him that Franklin had returned from Albany. He had tried to see Colden at Newburgh, but found no conveyance to Coldenham. He had left with Alexander the folio of minutes from the congress. Apparently Alexander had hoped to detain him long enough to plan a campaign among the colonies in behalf of the union. The defeat at Fort Necessity and Colonel George Washington's capture by the French upset the plan.

"We had news from Ohio you'll see in the public papers. It hastened the Pennsylvania commissioners [Franklin and] Peters from here, by several days sooner than they intended. They are in hopes their assembly now will join heartily in assisting Virginia—ours here is proposed to meet the third Tuesday of August, to provide for our own security at least; but [I] doubt whether anything will be done, by reason of the late instruction."

"I saw nothing else material in their whole proceedings, and am very well pleased they have agreed on these two things, which I hope may prevail on King and Parliament either in that or some better way to unite the force of the colonies, and that at the first meeting of parliament. . . .

"There's no more care taken of the five nations till another congress, than there used to be; they [the Iroquois] strongly called for their affairs being put in Col. Johnson's hands, but were answered they must be content with the commissioners of Indian Affairs for another year.

"I believe the DeLancey commissioners' endeavors is more to encourage the trade to Canada than in securing the Six Nations—an evident mark of it is, that they had been (when his honor came to the administration) not so much as notified that they had a commission to the five nations, nor given them any invitation to correspond with them, though that was many months after they had accepted the commission, when a positive order was sent to them by his honor's council [Alexander] to notify and invite."

The last paragraph, in its structure, shows signs of Alexander's distress over the failure of this first highly commissioned continental congress. Kept absent, probably by the gout, he had sent his son William as his proxy, and had done what he could, in his capacity as senior councillor and chairman of its committee on Indian affairs, to maintain protocol with the sensitive Indian chieftains. As usual, he blamed no one in particular, but it is easy to supply the name.

With Washington's capture, though neither side had formally declared war, the die was cast; the utopian Albany Plan was relegated to the pigeonhole of interesting ideas. The provinces were no more willing to consider it seriously than was Parliament. Alone in the provinces, James Alexander secured from New Jersey a favorable vote in both Council and Assembly, and a word of encouragement from the Council in New York. DeLancey had won his first round.

The way now lay open for further French successes, for DeLancey's profitable prolongation of the conflict, and for the final initiating of British rule of the colonies under a kind of martial law.

Yet though the Albany Plan was forgotten, Alexander's deep concern for union had been impressed upon the younger leaders of his day. The idea of union had been made familiar. Men had taken sides upon it. A Congress of the Provinces had been held, common interests communicated, and mutual jealousies exposed. Parliament's indifference, the opposition of American Tories, and the control of Indian nations and territories, stood out as hazards in the channel. Only if conditions should worsen could the mutual sense of injustice bring about the desired union.

After the Albany Congress, Pownall returned to Philadelphia with Franklin and Peters. He had agreed to aid Alexander's friend, Lewis Evans of Philadelphia, in the preparation of a map of the northern colonies. Evans had been encouraged by his work on Alexander's *Bill in Chancery* to extend his map making. In 1749 Evans had made his first map of the Provinces of New York and New Jersey, Pennsylvania and Delaware, with Alexander's assistance. He wrote Dr. Colden at the time,

"My map is finished at last and now waits upon you for your amendments; which if you could favor me with by the first opportunity, would oblige me much; for I wait now to have Mr. Alexander's and your revisal before I proceed to print them off."

Three years later Alexander tried to find an accurate map of New York alone, and could not recollect that he had ever seen any. He added, "Evans' map gives the lines of the counties well enough."

Alexander had realized the value in public relations which would be earned by such a map as Evans' of the four provinces; he had out of his great store of records provided the enthusiastic Welshman with essential data. Some of these appear in the delineation of the Oblong, in the Alexandrian version of the New York–New Jersey boundary line, and in the Cuyahoga boundary.

Pownall's employment by Evans occupied his summer and fall. By this time Alexander must have suggested to him an appointment as lieutenant governor of New Jersey. The act of appointment passed the following May; very promptly, all things considered.

Governor Jonathan Belcher of the Jerseys was ill; he had gratefully accepted from Alexander the loan of a medical work on the gout, by Doctor Cheney. He had suffered a mild palsy while attending the founding ceremonies of Princeton College, in 1754.

Alexander could thus hold out to young Pownall the pleasing prospect of early succession to a governor's seat. He hoped that real cooperation might develop between the ministry and the colonies. Thomas' brother John was the influential clerk of the Board of Trade. The two young men were favored by the inner circles of authority.

It was high time that some benign star should shine at last upon the distressed Dutch colonies. For DeLancey's claim to North Jersey had been timed to coincide with a threat by Hunterdon

County on the Jersey Delaware River, of secession to Connecticut.

As if this were not enough, the great land fever of the New England pioneers, caught from the contagious example of Elizabeth, was now in full strength. It contemplated nothing less than the acquisition by settlement and popular will of the whole of upper New York. Massachusetts speculators were already selling lots in townships erected by the Bay out of Livingston Manor. Alexander prepared the brief which DeLancey forwarded in protest to Governor Shirley. An evasive reply was returned.

Alexander advised Livingston to arm his tenants as he had done in Jersey; the action was taken with excellent results. The Boston men fled across the border.

As early as 1752, when the annulment of the Jersey north line became known, and Jersey's continuance was precarious, Connecticut speculators had taken advantage of the rising fever to consider a bolder "purchase" of the middle Hudson region, north of the Highlands.

From such a harebrained scheme, James Brown of Norwalk, the respected Connecticut attorney who had managed the Ridgefield sharers in the Thomas Hawley Company of 1730, and had acted ever since as their attorney, had dissuaded the reckless plungers in land-jobbing.

Brown was Alexander's faithful correspondent and warm friend. He had warned Alexander of what was brewing among the Connecticut farmers. They had now reached the Housatonic Valley in force, and were enraged with its rocks and swamps and steep hillsides. Green pastures lay beyond them.

Richard Peters soon wrote William Alexander of this crossing of the Delaware Jordan; the New Englanders were settling upon the Pennsylvania valleys like blackbirds, which returned as often as they were driven out, and finally overcame the previous owners of the woods. James Alexander wrote Robert Hunter Morris, now the governor of Pennsylvania, suggesting that he post rangers on the Pennsylvania frontier to warn Connecticut off. "A penny spent to nip the affair in the bud would save many pounds thereafter," he remarked. Twenty years later his prophecy was fulfilled in the Pennamite Wars. It is likely indeed that except for Alexander's open threat to the Hartford charter, south Jersey would have gone the way of Wyoming. Governor DeLancey was at the time encouraging such a step, and even offering to supply the money to influence Parliament in their behalf. He suggested that, if Connecticut could add south Jersey to its charter, he would then buy the whole "right" of northern New Jersey.

So at least Alexander was informed by James Brown. He had no reason to doubt this loyal and efficient aid. DeLancey worked on the theory that men had their price. Meanwhile the Connecticut farmers were flocking in crowds to the General Court of Connecticut, which granted them townships in both New York and Pennsylvania.

The "Flight of the Blackbirds" was, after all, inevitable. New England could no longer feed them, for there had been no agricultural preparation for dealing with worn-out pastures and fields. Their church control of the parish lands had also hindered their "hiving out," until it exploded.

Alexander kept Brown supplied with the familiar arguments. Connecticut claims of a "right" as far as the South Sea, in the gay nonchalance of King Charles's charter, could not stand against the solid fact that the Hudson was a Dutch river in 1662, when the charter was signed. King James II's grant to New York was just as valid in 1664.

But these people were beyond logic. The population explosion had come; they wanted out, to the west, which began at the Hudson shore.

The gathering of the Indian sachems at the Albany Congress was the golden opportunity for the land gamblers. There Connecticut announced to the astonished delegates that the colony had purchased the Wyoming Valley in the territory of Pennsylvania. Conrad Weiser, chief interpreter, angrily claimed that the transaction was illegal; the bargain had been made in a foul tavern, with the Indians too drunk to know what they had done.

Pennsylvania replied to Connecticut's threat by purchasing the Ohio region. Against both purchases Colonel William Johnson protested in vain. They had undone all the petty gains of the abortive Albany Plan, in alienating the Indian interest.

James Brown, in constant correspondence with Alexander at this time, bravely resisted the Connecticut schemers at home. He did so, in part at least, by encouragement of the Wyoming settlement.

Alexander's position, as manager of the proprietary company of the Jerseys, and attorney for the Penns' rights there, was a delicate one. He was in full correspondence with his former pupil, Robert Hunter Morris, who returned from England in 1754 as governor of Pennsylvania. The Penn proprietary still exercised its political right, and appointed him to fight the Wyoming battle.

The councillor knew well his Connecticut negotiators. "They will amuse and give good words till a great number be settled, then bid defiance," he told Morris. He was familiar with what a New Yorker called "the melancholy enthusiasm of the New Englanders."

Alexander's most telling argument, which he included in his

letters to Brown as well as to President Clapp of Yale, was that the colony was endangering her own charter by such frequent appeal to it as justifying the invasion of a peaceable neighbor. The word "charter" in Connecticut had magic in it; the loss of it was a sobering thought.

Alexander's point was immediately strengthened when Pownall was appointed lieutenant governor of the Jerseys. Alexander's defense became notably bolder in 1755, for Pownall was eager to cooperate.

The Connecticut Legislature finally refused to grant Hunterdon County the status of a New England one. This broke the back of the plan to occupy West Jersey in the New England polity.

Throughout the Connecticut-Susquehanna affair, William Alexander helped his father. He wrote a pamphlet on the claims. It was at his suggestion that James Hamilton of Philadelphia wrote Sir William Johnson on March 19, 1754, informing him that Connecticut was trying to corrupt the Iroquois nations and their subjects, and seize the Susquehanna region. This was four months before the purchase of Wyoming.

Governor Morris had been completely frustrated by Franklin in the Assembly, and had appealed to Alexander, who could only advise him to use his militia power, and station rangers along the Delaware to oppose the flow of settlers. But Franklin had frustrated this attempt also. He wanted more good English stock to people his province; no more tight Germans and testy Scots.

Wyoming became a "new Connecticut" for the next thirty years, organized as a county of the Yankee province. The stubborn New Englanders held their ground as Elizabeth did, until Mr. Franklin changed his mind, and as governor arrested his namesake, John Franklin, for trespass on the Pennsylvania boundary. He soon relented. The Yankees lost their county, however, and became loyal Pennsylvanians in the second generation. Some good came out of all this evil, to quote Parson Taylor of Newark.

On the other hand, Alexander also won his victory. He had maintained existing institutions. He had preserved the integrity of New Jersey, the boldest and the most truly democratic of the eastern states. He had done this without aid from London.

In his *Government of the Colonies,* Pownall wrote in 1764 in England:

"For until a practical and efficient administration be formed, whatever the people of this country may think, the people of the colonies, who know their business much better than we do, will never believe government to be in earnest about them or their interest, or even about governing them; and will, not merely from that reasoning, but from the necessity of their circumstances, act commonly.

"The people of the colonies say that the inhabitants of the colonies are entitled to all the privileges of Englishmen; that they have a right to the legislative power; and no commands of the Crown are binding upon them, farther than they please to acquiesce under such; that this right is inherent, and essential to the community, as a community of Englishmen."

This sounds like a quotation from Zenger's *Journal,* not from the Pennsylvania *Gazette.* It was not for nothing that Pownall spent a lot of time among Alexander's records and books, and at his fireside. There, and not in Boston or Philadelphia, the Swedish traveler Peter Kalm found the talk of union and independence.

Never were fireside talks more fruitful of lasting effects. During the dozen years between the Stamp Act and the Declaration of Independence, Pownall's voice was raised in defense of liberty more frequently than any other in England. The six editions of *The Government of the American Colonies* presented the colonial cause with increasing flavor and fullness at each reprint.

Alexander's "germ of freedom" had taken deep root in the mind of this ambitious young placeman, and stirred him almost into statesmanship.

Pownall refers to his American authorities as "the ablest lawyers of the country." In talking of commerce he makes mention of "a very great practitioner of the law of trade." It is not difficult to divine this person. In his discussion of the American courts he quotes from William Smith's *History of New York*, which was being written out of Alexander's records while Pownall was harboring in the hospitable house.

No other American would have given him the whole American philosophy of government. Franklin and he talked electricity, as we have seen. The younger men were jealous of him; his elders thought he wanted "to feed in my pasture", as DeLancey put it. He may have caught hints from the moot courts of the Alexander circle of young lawyers, of questions that he later wrote upon: "the suspense clause; should it be abolished?" "Shall America or England decide what laws shall be introduced from the common law?" "Is a New England charter of right stronger than others?"

Although Pownall joined Lord North in a last attempt to stave off the coming conflict, he did not abandon his confidence that nothing could stop independence. In December, 1777, he told a jeering House of Commons that the war was lost, and that the navigation acts were dead and gone. It was a most courageous action; a wreath laid on the altar of memory of an American friendship.

CHAPTER XIII

The affairs of war

THE YEAR 1755, fateful for James Alexander, opened in a cold war. From Connecticut James Brown was still writing of the spread of the "Blackbirds," and of his efforts to discourage them —vain, as yet, for the spirit was upon them. John Stevens was hard at work, driving against the rioters in Essex and Monmouth, and even into the rebel capital, Elizabeth. The Proprietors' war, in its last stages, was nearly ended; only the mopping up was left. The Jersey frontier was still at stalemate.

Alexander was already deep in the affairs of war. He had staked his son William in a partnership with Lewis Morris II and Peter Van Brugh Livingston, for supplying the English armies. They had established storehouses in Albany and Schenectady, to hold the wheat from Mrs. Alexander's sloops, and others.

Governor William Shirley of Massachusetts was already well known to New York circles; the originator of the successful Louisburg expedition in 1745, he had mobilized colonial supplies for the expedition and the ships to carry them. James Alexander at this time was the active power behind the governorship of New Jersey. By cautionary inference it would appear that he helped Governor Shirley in his work. He wrote at the time to Colden,

"The Boston expedition against Cape Breton, seems a bold undertaking. I heartily wish it may succeed, but I am afraid of it, for the want of warriors, and engineers, which I look upon to be as much an art as any manual occupation. . . . If it succeeds it will be the most glorious thing that has been done this war, and the most useful, if the conquest can be kept; for it's the only place of rendezvous that the French have to annoy the northern plantations with, from the sea."

In the following year when the British Government projected

its continental plan for a general assault on Canada, Alexander equipped and dispatched the New Jersey regiment with a speed that excited the envy of the other colonies. Shirley must have become acquainted with Alexander at this time, for he made himself familiar with the problems of politics in both the Middle Colonies. The disturbances in Boston which followed the capture of Louisburg led Shirley to think of resigning, and he applied for his appointment to the governorship of both New York and New Jersey on the terms which had preceded their separation.

On a leisurely voyage down the Hudson in 1748 with Admiral Clinton, Governor Shirley offered to help his fellow governor out of his DeLancey distress. In a six-weeks' stay in New York City he talked with the leading men; the outcome—probably Alexander's work—was a coalition of Colden and Clinton against DeLancey. Two years later Alexander joined them on the New York Council.

Now in the spring of 1755 Shirley and Alexander met again. Thomas Pownall, rather indiscreetly, confided to Alexander that he had delivered to DeLancey a letter from Boston; Shirley had engaged to put his strength into an expedition against Crown Point. The French had held it for twenty years; it was a perpetual threat to Albany. DeLancey, for his own good reasons, kept the letter to himself. Alexander managed to let the leaders of the legislature hear about it. They had refused to join in the war plans up to that time, fearing more diversions to Cap Breton. When the house met, such a disposition appeared to join in the scheme proposed, that it was out of DeLancey's power to obstruct it.

William Alexander made a map of the Champlain region of Crown Point, which was given to Pownall to print, of course anonymously. That young man got his own name on it; he was already the patron of Evans' larger map.

On his return to New York from General Braddock's council of war at Alexandria, April 13, 1755, Governor Shirley, now deputy commander in chief, stayed some days to arrange the purchase of military supplies. He hoped to compete for these as well as for militia with Colonel William Johnson, appointed to lead the Crown Point task force; he was himself to attack Niagara, a new plan. At a conference with Alexander and his former ally Robert Hunter Morris, now governor of Pennsylvania, it was decided that militia hitherto restricted to Crown Point, should be released "as well for Niagara as for Crown Point. They all agreed to go with New England and New York wherever His Majesty would."

Alexander did his utmost to aid Shirley. He diverted the Jersey regiment to the general's command. But he was embroiled with DeLancey over the boundary line; no help there. Pennsylvania was a vain hope. Benjamin Franklin, who hated all Penn appointees, sabotaged all Morris' efforts, though the governor offered him the command of a provincial army.

Worst of all, Governor Shirley had raised against himself the two strongest men of the time: James DeLancey and Sir William Johnson. He had chosen Johnson as the commander against Crown Point. DeLancey thought himself the proper man for the job. The Point was in New York, but Shirley was sending New England troops to take it. This could only mean that New England would eventually take over the Adirondack region.

Shirley had chosen Niagara for his own task force. DeLancey suspected that Massachusetts was about to substantiate her claim to the western lands of New York and to the hegemony of the Iroquois, a New York prerogative. Johnson's influence with the Indian nations over the whole western frontier was thus discarded, and Johnson himself tucked away in the Champlain country.

All this DeLancey looked upon with extreme disfavor. By conspiring with the Albany clique, his personal connections, he could effectively block Shirley's invasion of New York. And now came the worst of Shirley's offenses to plague him: James Alexander had tied up with General Shirley in a company of supply. His own son was a partner, his son-in-law Peter Van Brugh Livingston another, his closest associate Lewis Morris, Jr., the third. Already Shirley had snubbed his brother Oliver DeLancey's attempt to get contracts. The lieutenant governor fought back savagely. It seemed that Alexander had deliberately undertaken supply to thwart DeLancey's delays.

Young William Alexander's success in carrying out Shirley's orders for storehouses and supplies delighted the general. Shirley gave William the rank of major, made him his executive aide and private secretary, and withdrew him from the supply company. Plans were rapidly made for supplies from the storehouses at Albany and Schenectady, and Shirley, who was then past sixty years of age, took the field. The error of the campaign became at once apparent. Shirley could get no assurance of a peaceful passage through the Iroquois country to Niagara, and decided to confine his efforts to Oswego as the season advanced. Colonel Johnson, on the other hand, was floundering in the Adirondack forests with his New England levies and his unwilling Indians, on his way to Crown Point. Had their roles been reversed, complete success might have attended the campaign. In both armies the failure of logistics came near to being their destruction.

All this time Thomas Pownall was eating his heart out in inactivity in New York. For a time he became one of Shirley's messengers to the governors of other colonies for lack of some more important work. As he witnessed the failure of Shirley's Niagara hopes and the more serious errors in supply, he became suspicious of Shirley's abilities, and turned against him.

He was the more disposed to this because at Alexandria in April Shirley had ignored his young companion, and had even refused to introduce him to General Braddock. As the brother of the secretary of the Board of Trade and with other powerful connections at home, Pownall felt he should have been enlisted for the campaign in an important post. He eventually joined James DeLancey in active opposition to Shirley's campaign. James Alexander, more prescient than Shirley, had tried to find a place for Pownall, and it presently appeared that he would be made the lieutenant governor of New Jersey, thus adding strength to Alexander's direction of affairs during Belcher's incapacitation.

Alexander's influence with Shirley was shown in the general's selection of his personal staff. Captain John Rutherfurd, an intimate friend of the councillor and of Cadwallader Colden, was now appointed to the New York Council, and became a member of Shirley's military family. A second appointment was that of Captain Staats Long Morris, brother of Lewis Morris, who was serving with Braddock in his Virginia campaign and was later attached to Shirley's staff. Governor Robert Hunter Morris of Pennsylvania was, in fact though not in form, another member, loyally carrying out Shirley's recommendations.

None of these young men had had any experience in warfare, nor were their duties defined. William Alexander was acting not only as Shirley's confidential secretary and keeper of his records, but as engineer planning the fortifications of Fort Ontario at Oswego, and as commissary in full command of the supplies from the storehouses in Albany. In his letter of May 27 reporting to Shirley, he dealt with ship carpenters, firearms, provisions, bateaux and their crews, the so-called "battomen." He was also choosing camp-sites, erecting storehouses, securing headquarters, and gathering reports from spies, deserters, Indian traders, and others. No man, no matter how experienced, could exercise oversight on all these matters.

But this young man was also at work on the fort itself. He had made surveys of the whole way from Albany to Oswego, and was clearing out the waterways of rips and riffles, widening the portages, and building storehouses at the Great Carrying Place. Until Captain Bradstreet arrived, he would be in sole charge of designing and erecting the new fort.

"I heartily wish your Excellency could be there," he wrote, "for the Mohawk and Wood Creek grow shallow about the middle and latter end of the summer."

"There are no sailors to be had here," he went on. "If you can get twenty good ones from Boston, we may, I believe, make up the remainder at about 50 shillings a month.

"If the wind be fair," he added, "I shall set out for New York this afternoon."

It needs no great knowledge of the affairs of war to realize that James Alexander must have been very anxious about Shirley's management. Confined as he was by recurrent attacks of gout, he could only plan from his armchair to try to patch up some of the weak points in the campaign.

It was not long before his concern was deepened. In late July came the news of General Braddock's disaster on the Monongahela. Alexander had no time for vain regrets for what had happened. He realized at once that General Shirley, for the time being at least, would become commander in chief. James would give him what aid and counsel he could.

Braddock's depleted forces, under command of the highest surviving officer, Colonel Dunbar, had retreated the whole length of Pennsylvania with great alacrity, and were to go into winter quarters near Philadelphia.

Alexander convened the New York Council, and represented to General Shirley that such a step would be fatal. The regiments, though greatly reduced, were still a force in being.

Alexander urged that Albany, with its stores and strategic position, should be reinforced. General Shirley approved, and gave the order.

But at this, Governor Dinwiddie protested. The French would now attack Virginia. General Shirley countermanded his order. New York again protested. The troops finally reached Albany, leaving a garrison on the Schuylkill.

Alexander at once mapped out two important projects. The immediate danger to New York and New Jersey was their undefended frontier along the Delaware. Pennsylvania lay open to invasion. He therefore projected a joint expedition of the three colonies, not depending on the Crown, but by raising an independent force of their own.

The militia would march to the Delaware River frontier to meet any sudden incursion. They would set up blockhouses at distances of five miles, with small posts that would give the warning to militia forces in a second line, all under a single commander. For this post Alexander chose Charles Clinton of Ulster. He had done much work in surveying for the councillor, and was known to be a competent and courageous captain of militia.

Alexander's second project was the extension of the system of supplies to the British Army. He was already in touch with General Shirley, and interested in his son's company. This would be entirely insufficient to handle the amounts needed. Moreover, his son was already being withdrawn from the supply business, to manage Shirley's measures of defense.

To gain the cooperation of other companies a congress of supply would be necessary, for an effective union of organization, and for issuing the orders and contracts among the various provinces of New England and the middle region. Using the proxy of friends in the New Jersey Assembly, he addressed General Shirley.

"Sundries of the assembly heartily wish that a congress of commissioners should meet with General Shirley at Albany or where else he would be pleased to appoint in October or November next to agree on the further necessary supplies and forces for next year, that should be provided in the winter, so that all might be at the place of rendezvous by the first of the spring; that the commissioners should be appointed by acts of the several legislatures; but as they [the Jerseyites] are one of the smallest colonies they durst not take it upon them to begin a proportion for that purpose, but will most readily follow the other greater colonies so far as their abilities can go."

Alexander tried in his statesmanlike letter to make clear that the congress of commissioners would in no way usurp the powers of the commander in chief in the field. It would be a purely civilian operation. They would be told what kind of troops, infantry, artillery, cavalry, would be used; what sort of transport would be needed—water, land, mountain, plain, portage, or transport—and would then prepare and collect the goods, and settle the costs. In short, they would constitute the service of supply in a modern army.

Meanwhile the Iroquois nations, left to themselves by Johnson's war journey, decided to take a share in despoiling the Pennsylvanians. Some of them joined the Shawnees in the invasion of the Quaker province. Action was imperative.

By September of 1755 Alexander's plans were made. With a touch of the old fighter of the Cosby days, he wrote Colden that there were many things to learn from the losses of the year, which could be used in planning the next.

He found great encouragement in the arrival of Sir Charles Hardy, an energetic naval officer, to replace DeLancey as governor. The son and grandson of admirals, he had every virtue except experience in managing a province.

DeLancey and his Council met him. The lieutenant governor in the most flattering terms urged Hardy's need of rest after his voyage—not too tactfully, it would seem to a naval man—and generously offered to take the whole burden of the war from him, if His Excellency would immediately appoint DeLancey to the command of the New York forces north of the Highlands. At this, says William Livingston in his account of the affair, James Alexander, next in rank to DeLancey, intervened with the suggestion that the Council would wish to advise His Excellency upon so important a step.

Sir Charles could see the point, and made no decision. DeLancey became his enemy. The governor did not wait to worry, but sailed to Albany. Sir Charles kept up his preference for Alexander's counsel.

He at once supported Alexander's views on the boundary questions, and approved Alexander's choice of Charles Clinton to command the militia that was to march at once to the defense of the boundaries.

In mid-September Pownall was notified by Governor Belcher that his installation at Elizabeth would take place. "Pray present my compliments to Mr. Alexander, and bring him with you when you come."

Pownall accepted with alacrity. Alexander and he stayed long enough to secure the approval from the Assembly of an order to the militia to march to the frontier to protect the settlers. Next day, on their return to New York, the scene was repeated at the New York Council. In all, three thousand militia marched to Minisink, in time to overawe the roving bands who were massacring at will.

Alexander's Cranberry Indians remained loyal, but the advocate feared that bands of the Shawnee and other Ohio Indians would invade not only the inland farms of Delaware and Susquehanna, but would cross over into New Jersey and New York. He wished to further Sir William Johnson's policy of reducing these dangers by regaining the confidence of the Iroquois. At the same time, he thought it possible that a strong defense along the Delaware would deter the occasional raiders.

There was an equal danger that the enraged white settlers might revenge themselves not only upon the raiding Shawnees, but on the resident Christian Indians. He had observed the disaffection of the Mohawks, at the conference in Albany in 1753, when Chief Hendrick had stalked out of the meeting declaring that the "covenant chain" was broken and null. He blamed DeLancey's Albany ring of traders. "They are devils," he shouted.

Alexander at once acted for the Cranberry Indians of New Jersey. They told him that they had refused the demands of the Delawares to join them. For this, they had been marked for destruction. On the other hand, Americans had begun to threaten them, merely for being Indians.

It speaks much for Alexander's civilized approach to the problem, that he obtained an act for the immediate registration of the whole Cranberry nation. Certificates would be provided them, warning all whites that they were under the governor's protection. To distinguish them in case of a sudden raid by "foreign" Indians, the Cranberry would each wear a red ribbon in the hair. The idea caught. At least, no record has been found of any such massacre as took place in the Quaker province. Other Indians in Jersey were also given shelter.

Alexander returned with Pownall to New York. He had scarcely arrived when his guest brought him a letter he had received from the famous Indian agent, Conrad Weiser in Pennsylvania, which conveyed the favorable news that dissension had broken out between the French garrison at Fort Duquesne and the Shawnee Indians. Two French soldiers, who had gone foraging too far from the fort, had been scalped. Supplies were evidently running low and the garrison was practically in a state of siege.

With Pownall in close association with him, and the Cranberry Indians provided for, he awaited Governor Shirley's reply with good hope.

Pownall had carried the letter for him, but Alexander had used the strictest protocol in forwarding the letter through the courtesy of Governor DeLancey. DeLancey would see in the letter Alexander's evident intention to throw open the provision of army supplies to all merchants in the trade. It would no longer be the monopoly of the Alexander group.

General Shirley received the letter and instantly adopted Alexander's plan. He named the councillor gratefully in a letter to the governors of the other colonies with a call for a Congress of Commissioners on the 15th of November.

The delays of the campaign, however, forced a postponement of the Congress to the second week of December. Shirley therefore sent the letter out on September 11th from Oswego, with an introduction scarcely calculated to help its success. The letter is to Josiah Willard of Boston.

"The thought of having a meeting with Commissioners from the Colonies in order to consult upon the most proper measures to be taken for the general interest of the common cause the next spring was suggested to me by the enclosed account given to Governor DeLancey by

Mr. Alexander, a member of his Majesty's Council for the provinces of New York and New Jersey; and as it seems to me a very desirable procedure, I desire his Honour would take the first opportunity of proposing it to the General Assembly for their consideration, and shall myself mention it to the Governors of all the other Colonies as far as Virginia inclusive for the consideration of their respective assemblies."

General Shirley was sixty-two years of age (the equivalent of seventy-five today). He was tired out after a fatiguing journey through the wilderness to Oswego. Thus he was in no state to issue Alexander's proposal as his own, to make it obligatory upon patriotic British subjects at that most critical time.

Naturally, the governors did not take Alexander's suggestion very seriously. They were, most of them, on the worst terms with their own Assemblies, and jealous of their interfering with the war. They had had the experience at Albany of seeing Governor DeLancey violate his own invitation by presiding at the Congress in 1754, the only governor present, while he had no chosen delegates himself from New York. They determined therefore, to attend the conference themselves, and to tell Shirley how to run the war, not to talk about flour and gunpowder and such petty items.

Thus Alexander's great plan, indispensable for success, went whistling down the wind. The Congress met, but only Connecticut and Rhode Island, two provinces not provided with frontiers, sent delegates. The Congress was deferred till November, then to December 12. Alexander kept at work, but gave up hope for any united effort from the colonies, unless Lord Halifax's plan, which was then in Parliament, should be adopted. He hoped it would "be good, and take place" by enactment. But it, too, failed to please anyone, though in itself reasonable and workable, under a strong administration.

In the meantime, Shirley's army bogged down completely; Johnson's in the foothills of the Adirondacks, had only six days' supplies. This in the midst of plenty, with storehouses filled with provisions. Alexander laid all the blame on the "villainous battomen," who had struck and fled home when they were neither clothed, fed, or paid.

That, apparently, was not William Alexander's fault, but the treasurer's, at Albany. But the evil was done, and the supplies could not move. It may be surmised that the DeLanceys made no effort to get things moving.

The noise of cannonading could be plainly heard near Albany, and presently came the welcome news of the capture of General Dieskau of the French Army, and the repulse of his forces. Colonel Johnson had redeemed the summer of failure.

Having set in operation the project of supply, Alexander could be of no further aid. He had looked eagerly to his proposed Congress, and entertained some of the delegates, including Pownall. But the governors had no need of his services, as they turned their meeting into a general staff.

He could still move to help the frontier. His first efforts in Pennsylvania had been thwarted. Governor Morris had been eager to aid; Colonel Benjamin Franklin, of the Philadelphia militia was not. He disliked proprietary power in any aspect. He arrived too late to save the Moravians at Gnadenhutten (Allentown) but erected three forts to defend Philadelphia. Thus General Shirley felt able to claim a line of defense posts from Fort Cumberland in Maryland as far as the New York frontier. At Fort Cumberland a young New Jersey wagoner named Daniel Morgan had his first brush with the Indians.

Alexander did what he could. With Pownall's personal aid, he had persuaded the Councils of New Jersey and New York to adopt almost identical resolutions. They would spare 265 men in New Jersey and 260 men in Orange and Ulster counties, New York, for a voluntary enlistment in defense of the Delaware line. In case of extreme need they might for a short distance cross the provincial boundary to give assistance. They were instructed by Alexander "to let no disputes about the location of the boundary lines interrupt their harmony." Here, indeed, was the union idea in practice, on home ground.

Both measures, he assured Colden, were obtained "by means of the application of Mr. Pownall." He went on to say, "I verily believe that if the militia of New Jersey and New York had not marched to the Delaware, Minisink would have been cut off by this time. There seems proof that it was their plan, after destroying Gnadenhutten, that Minisink would have been next."

But although Alexander had thus saved the Delaware islands, and with them Easton, a county seat on the western shore of Delaware, Colonel Franklin did not see fit to lay aside his dispute with the Penn heirs who still controlled the provincial government, as Alexander had laid aside his feud with the governor of New York.

Instead, Colonel Franklin, backed by the city Council that had chosen him to command their musters, and the General Assembly of the province, put off the frontiersmen and defied the governor, until the whole countryside was ravaged as far as the Schuylkill. Franklin went to England as the Assembly's agent, in June, 1757, to plead their cause against the Penns for the next three years, by which time the damage had been done.

Instead of reforming the Proprietors on a business basis, as Alexander had done, he tried to abolish them. The Penns, by a little sharp trading, kept nearly all their power.

New Jersey quickly manned the blockhouses erected, at least one in every five miles, up to Mahakamak. From there, New York took over, building forts for eighty miles to the north, as far as Rochester in the Shawangunk Valley.

Through the winter the joint defense worked well, but in February, when the exhausted rangers came home from their freezing vigil, care was relaxed, and forays began once more.

"If only the Assemblies act cordially toward the idea," Alexander wrote Colden, "I think you'll be safe from these attacks of the foreign Indians. I wish you were as safe from those neighbor Indians that frequent your house." In a postscript he added, "Keep a candle or lamp burning at night in an upper room."

He urged his friend to have greater care. "Admit no Indian beyond the kitchen. Let none carry knife or gun; if he does, treat him as an enemy. It is better to be on the side of caution and daring, than on the side of too much confidence and security." The next year, Colden's Indians all deserted him. Later, assaults came on the New York side; Colden's family fled to his residence on Long Island, whither Colden followed, to spend the rest of his useful life there.

Before he left Ulster County, he had carried out Alexander's request, that he secure the appointment of Charles Clinton as colonel of the frontier militia. Colonel Clinton already captained a company under Colonel DeKey. As James's surveyor, he had commended himself; as Bradstreet's second in command of militia, he was one of the few colonial officers to bear a good name at the end of the war. With him were his young sons: James as captain, George as lieutenant. Both were promising officers, and expert surveyors.

During this period, from February until May, the Assembly of New York had passed one bill after another, approving Alexander's plan for the joint defense of the frontier by New York, New Jersey, and Pennsylvania. In February four hundred rangers were authorized for an expedition "for the protection of our western frontiers, in conjunction with Pennsylvania and New Jersey, which were become fields of blood by the daily ravages of inhuman barbarities."

On March 2, the General Assembly voted "up to 1000 men to act in conjunction with New Jersey and Pennsylvania in an expedition against the castles and settlements of Indians, enemies to His Majesty's subjects of these colonies."

Apparently Shirley had interposed, to put the rangers under his command, and to use them in offensive war. This phrase occurs in an action of March 9. On March 8 Shirley wrote a letter home, boasting of his new bastion 500 miles in length. He had taken over Alexander's plan for publicity. Each outpost, he said, was manned by from seventy to a hundred men!

In May, 1756, the Assembly was still clinging to Alexander's rangers, but had weakened their control. "As soon as the frontiers are secure and the proposed expeditions with the colonies of New Jersey and Pennsylvania are at an end, the governor or commander-in-chief may augment the forces against Crown Point by 400 men."

All this must have given concern to James Alexander. He had pledged his good name in the venture. With extensive properties in Orange and Ulster counties, and with a house at Toby Mills, near Goshen, he was bound in honor to act as the elder statesman of the mid-Hudson community.

On March 15, it was brought to the attention of the House of Assembly, that James Parker and William Weyman, publishers of the New York *Weekly Postboy*, printed an article reflecting on the privilege of the Assembly. They were brought to the bar of the house (Weyman was absent at first), and confessed the fault, but pleaded error of judgment. They had, they said, excised several expressions they thought "indecent."

Upon interrogation, they stated that the article had been written by the Reverend Hezekiah Watkins of Goshen, who was notified to attend. His case, however, did not come up until October, 1756, when he pleaded his fault, committed under great excess of emotion. He was then reprimanded severely, and discharged.

The Reverend Mr. Watkins' article was mild enough, by modern standards. The militia had been called out again and again to repel raids. They had not been paid. Goshen petitioned later, for payment to them for their past sufferings.

"Six shillings per man would have been enough to provide sufficient troops to destroy the marauding Indians. . . . Although repeated applications have been made, we have been most cruelly neglected."

Colonel Charles Clinton and his fellow officers were in attendance. They and their men, according to the governor, had been on the watch all winter. They could not be everywhere, during the sudden attacks. Clinton left Goshen at once for a conference with James Alexander, at Toby Mills.

The case must have deeply affronted Alexander. He had just come from Goshen, the county seat of Orange, where he owned large tracts of land. Colonel Matthews of Goshen, then in the militia, had been his friend for many years. This arrogant conduct of DeLancey's Assembly would recall the chief justice's conduct twenty years before in John Peter Zenger's case. Prerogative again had challenged human rights.

Just before he began his examination of the distress on the frontier, there arrived an "express" from Sir William Johnson, containing the text of the treaties prepared for the Indian nations. To the Delawares he would restore their nationhood and their valleys; to the Iroquois he would engage not to sanction further cessions.

Alexander gave a day to their perusal, and made his observations before returning them to the express, who was probably an Indian runner. Then he turned once more to the matter in hand, examining and taking down depositions long after nightfall.

On March 24, immediately following his perusal of Sir William Johnson's treaties, Alexander went into conference at Toby Mills with Cadwallader Colden and Archibald Kennedy of the Council, and with Colonel Charles Clinton of the militia,

". . . concerning the miserable state of Orange and Ulster counties, and concerning the red men, before the council, which unless altered will in great measure depopulate and ruin [them]. I have two councillors agreed to attend commission tomorrow.

"March 25. Attended council at Catskill at 11. Bill for expeditions under consideration. Agreed to appoint a committee to examine into state of the counties of Ulster and Orange. Appointed 3 P.M. at my house. Sundry persons attended. Examined several of Goshen which took up till after dark.

"March 25. Notes. Letter from John Stevens. Governor promises him captaincy of the 51st."

The date of March 26, but no word, follows. His tireless pen wrote no more.

On April 2, after his arrival in Albany, the people's advocate died in "pain." He was still suffering acutely from his latest attack of gout.

He was buried in the family vault at New York.

The *New York Mercury*, in words more specific than was usual in its conventional eulogies, described "a gentleman in his disposition, generous, courteous, and humane, delicate in his sense of honor, steadfast in friendship, of strict probity, temperate in his diet, and in business indefatigable . . . "The relations of husband, father and master he sustained with the highest reputation : . . ." The writer, whom I take to be Dr. Colden, goes on to mention his very great researches in mathematics, his eminence in law, and his superior knowledge in public affairs.

Loyally serving in the highest stations, while "always true to the interests of his country," Colden marks him as the real patriot, "well knowing that the rights of the Crown are the bulwark of the liberties of the people, that the liberties of the people are the safety and honor of the Crown, and that a just proportion of both constitutes the health of the politic body . . ." Checks and balances again! The good doctor here pays tribute to the watchful engineer.

More simple, because more heartfelt, was the tribute of affection made by the Proprietors of East Jersey in their letter of condolence to Maria Alexander. Its shift from formal "they" to personal "we" proves the sincerity in which the friends wrote.

"When alive they esteemed him, they trusted him, they loved him. They have reason therefore, now he is taken from them, to bear part in your griefs, having lost their counselor, their friend, and their unwearied assistant.

"The Council, sensible of the manifold obligations his friendship and services have laid them under, think it their duty to assure the family, that we shall never cease to give them all the assistance in our power, for the completing of their titles, or recovering their rights in any lands of his in this Decision, or to do anything else which you shall be advised we can do for your benefit.

We are with great regard, Madam,
Your most faithful and obedient servants."

The Proprietors at their next meeting elected William Alexander to succeed his father as their Surveyor General. As he had been asked by General Shirley to accompany him to England, the Company made him their agent in England to present their cause.

CHAPTER XIV

A prevalence of lawyers

ALEXANDER'S REAL HERITAGE was a united group of men of very considerable ability, whom he hoped to see in power as the "Free Traders." He meant by the name an economic liberalism that would seek to continue his work for freedom in the fur trade and in the commerce with the West Indies and European lands and colonies.

They kept the old name of Whigs, however. Alexander died before the conquest of Canada was completed. He left no record of his vision beyond such an event; the role of prophet did not interest him.

But the logic of events determined that the other issue to which his life had been devoted, should be the keynote of the party he left behind. This was government, in union and in liberty.

His *Journal* articles and his public pamphlets were, of course, not revolutionary, but conservative on a basis of historic development. He clung to the true British constitution, and sought to replant it on American soil.

This became the cardinal creed of the American Whigs. With Alexander, they united the advocate's sense of history with a powerful appeal to the lovers of liberty in every class, but especially to the rural freeholders and the city artisans and laborers.

The same sort of people that rallied to the defense of John Peter Zenger were those who went to war with a political constitution in their saddlebags. The combination is unique in history. It was a revolution led by lawyers, and effected by them.

Cadwallader Colden in his Tory days warned the home government of this danger, from his post as lieutenant governor of New York. The turbulence that followed the Stamp Act, he wrote, was due to "the dangerous influence which the profession of the law has obtained in this province, more than in any other part of his Majesty's dominions." As usual his critical analysis was right, though he could only observe, not act upon it.

Colden's opposite number was William Smith, the historian, who spent his time before the outbreak of hostilities in designing one constitution after another in the hope that the war might thus be averted. He was still Whig enough to realize that there could be no taxation in America without representation. His own pupils, Robert R. Livingston, Gouverneur Morris, and George Clinton, were all prominent Whigs. His grandson, Peter R. Livingston, was America's first wealthy champion of the rights of labor. So effective was his heritage from Alexander. At the very last his pupil Morris begged Smith to "come over, where you belong."

He remained loyal, becoming chief justice of occupied New York, then of Quebec. There was no such hesitancy among Alexander's own family.

William, the only surviving son of Alexander, helped his mother, as is already related. The girls became notable housekeepers and beloved mothers. Alexander's appreciation of his wife was reflected in his will. He left everything to her, with the suggestion that she might, if she chose, make the same division of the estate as he would have done had she died before him; he then listed his own theoretical division.

His sons and sons-in-law worked closely with him and shared his ideas. William Alexander, though he adopted the title of Lord Stirling, at his friends' urging and after the verdict of a Scots jury, was nevertheless an ardent independent Whig. Stirling succeeded his father as surveyor general of the Jersey Proprietors and councillor in New York.

Peter Van Brugh Livingston, husband of daughter Mary, joined Stirling in the company that furnished Shirley with his supplies at Albany. To do so he borrowed from his wife's future inheritance. The deduction appears in Alexander's will. Peter Livingston went on to become a leader in the Liberty days. He was president of New York's first Provincial Congress. Ill health prevented further service, but he entertained John Adams on his official visit in rebel New York, and Adams left a pleasing picture of his fine house and hospitality.

John Stevens, husband of Alexander's daughter Elizabeth, aided him throughout his struggle to save the Proprietors. He continued as a leader in the growing province, serving on many commissions. He was president of the convention which ratified the United States Constitution, while his son John wrote a persuasive pamphlet in its favor. Interested in surveying and other branches of engineering, he left a large estate, and a heritage of invention and science that made a famous name.

Elisha Parker, husband of his daughter Catherine, was destined by Alexander to succeed him as surveyor and counsel for the Company of Proprietors, but died while yet assistant counsel. His widow, after his death, married in 1758 Major Walter Rutherfurd, brother of Captain John Rutherfurd. Both men were greatly interested in the colonies. John died at Ticonderoga. Walter purchased an estate at Niagara, an indiscretion that aroused Indian resentment. At the Revolution, still a moderate Tory, he was given house arrest, but not exiled or deprived of his property. His son John, like all Alexander's grandsons, was an ardent patriot.

These were his direct heirs, son and sons-in-law. The most active sons of his intellectual principles belonged to the great families whose attorney or colleague he had been for so many years: Livingston, Morris, Clinton, Smith, and Colden.

With most of them he was also allied in marriage. Judge Robert R. Livingston of Clermont, whom he had chosen to lead the Whig party, had an even more famous son, Chancellor Robert R. Livingston, who married Mary Stevens, his granddaughter. Lord Stirling had two daughters. Mary married the son of John Watts, brother-in-law of DeLancey and Tory leader of the Assembly, a moderate who served two more terms after the war. Catherine married William Duer, of the Continental Congress, assistant secretary of the treasury under Washington. All these complex strands wove together a power in the state, in the light of the advocate's ideas.

The proof of the permanence of the heritage is to be guessed from four great-grandsons: Livingston, Rutherfurd, Stevens, and Provoost, all christened James Alexander.

Nothing is more striking in this heritage than the inheritance of dissent in the several fields of Alexander's career that ran through all the heirs of his ideas. They may be classified under five heads: leaders of independency and makers of the Constitution; leaders in industrial arts and public service; and leaders in religion and education. To them a sixth class may be added; the moderate Tories, whose sons remained American, and continued their leadership.

The careers of these men fill other volumes, and will only be briefly mentioned here. Though they had close association in the Alexander family, they are not claimed as mere pupils, but as men who, growing up in a certain climate of opinion, continued the heritage in their own way.

The three Williams, Smith, Livingston, and Stirling, were associated in the affairs of Jersey long before their teacher's death. William Smith, Jr., read deeply in his library, and published several of his best-known addresses. He shared with Livingston in writing the famous New York address to Governor Colden, where the expression "not to be taxed without our own consent," first appeared in official legislation. Livingston and Stirling collaborated in the defense of General Shirley. The *Review of the War* loyally describes several occasions on which James Alexander thwarted Governor DeLancey's efforts to obstruct the progress of the campaigns. The young authors continued to work closely together in the legislature, and in pamphleteering. Livingston and William Smith together edited the laws of the province, and led the "Sons of Liberty." They headed the opposition to the Stamp Act, in the New York Legislature, while Stirling was raising a company of grenadiers to resist the sale of stamps by force.

In 1772 Livingston moved to New Jersey, where he and Stirling became neighbors. At the Revolution Livingston was chosen governor; Stirling raised regiments and became a general in the Continental forces under Washington, who made him his wing commander, and assigned to him important duties in erecting forts and other defenses. After service throughout the war Stirling died in January, 1783, while in command of a northern army and the line against Canada. His military record in battle had been admirable; he had lived with Washington "in the strictest bonds of amity," to quote the grave Virginian.

His daughter Kitty was the wife of William Duer, an active member of the Continental Congress and a strong adherent of Washington in trying times. The Duers entertained Lord Stirling overnight on his way to the northern command, when the house was assailed by Tory tenants of Rhinebeck. The beleaguered household made a successful defense.

An intimate of the Duers was Gouverneur Morris, who with Duer kept watch over Washington's interests in the Congress. With the other young Livingstons and Stirlings at Liberty Hall and Basking Ridge they made a gay party. There were four lovely daughters. It was Kitty Alexander who danced the quadrille with the father of his country at his inaugural ball. Her husband worked closely with Alexander Hamilton. Miss Livingston married John Jay, who with Robert R. Livingston, Jr., represented the legal heritage from Alexander.

Morris' great contribution was in the Constitutional Convention, where he was Washington's right hand, as Stirling was in the army. When the convention ended, it was Morris who gave the great document its style, and wrote the entire preamble. By the College of Electors he saved the Congress from being the choice of legislatures, and he worked for a strong judiciary, but neither he nor Jay won the battle over slavery.

Bishop Samuel Provoost, independent and courageous rector of Trinity, chaplain of the Senate, first bishop of New York, was a most grateful gift to the sadly depleted church. Many of its clergy had been active Tories. William Alexander Duer, a great-grandson, also a rector, became the sixth president of Columbia College, and the author of his namesake's biography.

John Stevens, Jr., grandson of Alexander, and Robert R. Livingston were brothers in science as well as in law. Neighbors on the Hudson and equally absorbed in experimental development of the steamship, their mutual story is too well known to repeat. The Chancellor wrote a speech for his nephew, little James Alexander Stevens, to recite at his school commencement, which won admiration at the time.

It was Livingston who urged his friend George Clinton to permit the cession by New York of her claims to western lands (the old Cuyahoga treaty). Clinton approved, and a chain reaction followed that caused a Northwest Territory to be created. This brought on the Federal Constitution. At the Poughkeepsie convention Clinton was chairman, Livingston the keynote speaker and advocate.

Judge David Ogden, Alexander's partner and brother-in-law of Gouverneur Morris, had a law pupil, Richard Stockton, who trained in his own office the great Jersey Federalists: Elias Boudinot, William Paterson, and Joseph Reed, the leader in Pennsylvania. A patron of Princeton, Stockton secured John Witherspoon for Princeton, under whom James Madison learned his Federal A B C.

John Rutherfurd, another of Morris' brothers-in-law, was president of his grandsire's Board of Proprietors, and their staunch supporter. A member of the Jersey Legislature, he was among the first presidential electors, and served as U.S. Senator from 1791 to 1798. With Morris, his intimate friend, he worked on New York's commission that planned its growth beyond Fourteenth Street; with him he received the city's freedom, as his grandfather had been honored.

This summary list of some of James Alexander's heirs of his great dissents makes no claim either to a monopoly of them, or to their predominance in the sequence of events. The history of ideas always leads back to multiple sources.

Nor is there any claim to originality in Alexander's stock of ideas. If there is uniqueness in his intellectual heritage, it lies in the fact that he brought with him a Scottish background of study, a discipline of navy service, a library of law, and a mind eager to demonstrate the validity of the legal approach to the solution of the basic American problem—the creation of a substitute for an outworn colonial system.

The conflict with the abuses of colonialism has often been described by historians in terms of the struggles of provincial assemblies against governors, and of the consequent withering away of the councils. This was not true of the Dutch colonies.

Alexander in New Jersey, and DeLancey in New York, led the Assembly from their seats in Council, and not infrequently the governor as well.

It was Alexander's unique gift as councillor for more than forty years, that he sought also to create among the three powers of government a system of checks and balances. His success made joint colonial action possible, and with this union came the hope of liberty.

When union came after the Revolution these states were well balanced in their divided powers: with strong governors, trained senators, and vigorous assemblies. Each state had developed an ample reservoir of leadership.

General Washington's chief support among the state governments came from the neighbor states of Connecticut, New York, and New Jersey.

Yet although Alexander counseled union for twenty years, he had also emphasized the importance of the self-reliant state. Only a jealous Board of Trade in London obstructed his march toward colonial autonomy.

There was room even in a colonial system, he taught, for full authority at every level of government, so long as each organ of the body politic moved freely in its own functions. This balance it was the responsibility of every part to maintain in harmony with the rest; an engineer's "tolerance." He worked at the same time for union among the provinces in matters of common concern; peace and war, trade and commerce.

Injustice at the top, disloyalty at the bottom, would otherwise grow, cell-like, in their harmful spread. Only an organism healthy in all its parts could resist peril.

Alexander fought to the end against usurpation by every legal means in his power, and perished gallantly in the struggle. He left behind a heritage of dissent, that established the great Republic.

Notes

Page

1 New York's population, in round numbers: 1723, city 7,000 colony 40,500; 1731, city 8,600, colony 50,300; 1746, city 11,700, colony 61,600; 1756, city 13,000, colony 96,800. NYDH, I, 691-97. New Jersey population: 1726, 32,400; 1745, 61,400.

2 He is said to have sailed from London, and landed in New York, August 17, 1715. Fish, *Pedigree*, 81-83; Smith, *History*, I, 23 f.

He met on the voyage William Smith, later his partner.

Tireless worker:

Docket, 1721–45 in N.Y. Supreme Court and Mayor's Court, "Follows a dogget of all causes I have been concerned in depending in New York Supreme Court whereof the costs have not been paid before Jan. 1725–6 and continued after." NYHS, Box 10.

Docket—Opinions. In addition to the cases in Supreme Court, a list of 60 "opinions" is included, (57-59) with costs. One of these was for John Burnet, on the settlement of Governor Burnet's will (1738).

In addition to the hundreds of cases in New York Supreme Court, there are even more in the catalog of the clerk of the Supreme Court at the State House, Trenton, N. J.

Rapid promotion:

Offices in New Jersey:

Surveyor general, Nov. 7, 1715. NJA, XIV, 3. Receiver general and collector of quitrents [for N.J. Proprietors] April, 1716. NJA, XIV, 241-42.

Recorder of Perth Amboy, 1718, B.P. *MSS*. He wrote the city charter.

Council—appointment July 19, 1722, oaths September 26, 1723. NJA, V, 52-53; V, 245.

["Has served two years as deputy secretary at New York with great approbation with Brigadier Hunter."] Burnet to Lords of Trade, NYDCH, V, Nov. 26, 1720. Hunter left New York in June, 1719; thus "two years" places his term as deputy secretary in 1717.

Attorney general, 1724; resigned December 27, 1727. NJA, XIV, 347. ["I cannot charge myself with neglect of the King's interest on the one hand . . . or with any oppression of the subject on the other, nor with receiving any fees whatsoever but what are appointed."]

Offices in New York (the same governor until 1738) Council: nominated Nov. 26, 1720, by Burnet; appointed August 3, 1721. NYDCH, V, 982 n. Attorney general, July 28, 1721; resigned March 17, 1723. NYDCH, 982 n. Naval officer, June, 1723–33. *Ibid.* Absent from Council, 1732–50 (by "omission"). Reinstated in New York Council by mandamus August 2, 1750. N.Y. Council *Minutes*, XXI, 403.

Alexander is also referred to by Burnet as advocate general of New York, appointed July 28, 1721. N.Y. *Boundaries*, II, 608.

3   High School of Stirling. Alexander home was at Menstrie near Stirling at the foot of the Ochil range of hills. It was a property of the Argylls from 1505. Rogers, *Stirling*, Chapter 14.

Old Pretender. The Scottish Act of Union in 1707 gave him his chance to rebel. On the Jacobite rebellion in 1707 and hunger in Scotland see Mathieson, *Union*, 9.

Jacobites. It would be tempting to describe James Alexander as an angry young man. He was born into the austerity of "the Killing Time." William III was a savior in England, but a ruthless oppressor in Scotland. The massacre at nearby Glencoe was one of many incidents.

Arundel. Alexander's refusal, NYDCH, V, 321. The ship's log is in the Rutherfurd Collection, NJHS. Scottish Jacobites. Insh, *Jacobites*, 87.

4   Whigs came back. Law as a substitute for the force of war or rebellion was the central Whig policy. Governor Hunter first expressed it in America: "A government of laws." Alexander made it the motto of his life and bequeathed it to his heirs.

Councilman, New Jersey, *N.Y. Col. Docs.*, V, 698. Notice July 9, 1723; appointed September 26, 1723 (dated February 28, 1723). NJA, II, 244, 245; NJA, III, 84. For Argyll's personal interest, *Duer*, 5.

His father. For the genealogy see Rogers, *Stirling*, 115. Livingston Rutherfurd, genealogy, *Fam. Records, House of Lords Journal*, XXX, 186. Colden *Papers*, V, 159. Robertson, *Scots Peerage*, 286, 306 (1740).

5   His own name. Andrew Alexander was a settler in 1685. His sons George and John, were well settled on the Raritan River. NJA, II, 204; BP, I, 83, etc. "Mr. George Alexander, Advocate," was a British Proprietor. BP, I, 234.

Library catalog. Listed in his Inventory of 1720 made just before his marriage. NJHS.

Byerley, Thos. Resistance to Cornbury, NYDCH, IV, 1142.

Perth Amboy (named for the Earl of Perth). Scots settlers had read the pamphlet of Robert Scott, *Model of the Government of East Jersey, 1685.*

Gordon, Thos. Gordon, *New Jersey*, 32-48.

Col. Hunter's motto: "It is better to make an end of all disputes than to delay them." *N.Y. Boundaries*, II, 600.

6 Palatinate. The "poor Palatines" were settled on Staten Island and the upper Hudson. W. A. Knittle, *Early Palatine Emigration (1936)*; Leder, *Livingston*, 204, 212-13, 220-26.

Vegetian manner. *Vegetius on War*, IV, the ancient and still classical authority.

7 Westward empire. New England's claims to the West derived from Charles II's grant of 1662 "as far as the South Sea." Although quite mythical, the claim was loudly sustained as late as 1800, becoming the basis of claims to land in central and western New York and even the Western Reserve of Ohio.

9 Alexander, estimate by Wm. Smith, 1760. *History*, I, 231. "A gentle man conversant with the law and equally esteemed for his generosity, humanity, great abilities, and honorable stations."

Colony records and Indian treaties bound in four large volumes. NYDCH, V, 982-83 n. Smith *History*, I, 214.

To peruse and to examine. With Alexander, to peruse was to read closely. Examination was a more thorough legal process. His "thoughts" are notes in his *Daybooks* for future development in the improvement of legal and official processes.

10 Colden wrote to an inquirer of Alexander: "Mr. Alexander is a man of very considerable estate and great honor, with whom you may safely deal." *Colden*, II, 251, 1741.

"Indefatigable." *Colden*, IX, 328.

Bill from DeLancey, 1756. Itemized list of fees, 1733–56. Fees due Chief Justice for cases on his docket £1542 2 s. submitted by Oliver DeLancey, 1741. James Alexander was paid £60 s. 6 d. on March 2, 1741 (possibly Chesecock patent N.Y.–N.J.) List of cases before the Chief Justice 1735–56 for fees to the Chief due from James Alexander, 337 cases at 10 s. each, total £168.10.

There are perhaps 200 more in the Catalog of Cases for 1715 in the office of the archivist at the State House, Trenton, N. J. Many others are listed in the Minutes of the Supreme Court in the clerk's office.

Hunter. Hunter's good sense appears in his statement of principle: "The true interests of the people and the government are the same: a government of laws." NJA, II, 36.

11 Hunter's opponents. The Jacobite party had passed a law making belief in the Trinity requisite for voting. Alexander remarked, "The

Inquisition was nothing to this." Hunter had good cause to dissolve the Assembly. Ruth. Coll., IV, 15; NJA, V, 55-63.

Survey. Alexander's *Map of N.J.*, NJA, V, 188. London Board, Letter from NJA, IV, 241-42.

12 Dod. NYCM, *Alexander MSS.*

Dod, poem quoted in *N.Y. Gazette*, December 30, 1729. *Arts and Crafts in New York*, 179, 180.

Alexander wrote Col. Hunter in 1725 of an attempt by Dr. Johnston, a kinsman of DeLancey, to replace the Proprietors by an intrigue. It was defeated by David Ogden. NJA, V, 55.

13 Alexander, after ten years of unsatisfactory management of the great property to please the whims of a board of directors in London, now took a long step in the attainment of economic independence. The Earl of Stair made him his proxy with full power to vote his shares. Others took the same course. With the Morris family support, enough American shares were found to constitute an American Board of Directors. On March 25, 1725, the new board was organized by the adoption of a constitution. The purpose, stated in the first article, was to effect "a firm and strict union of the Proprietors." Any proprietors with even a one-eighth share, by ownership or proxy for a sufficient number of proxies, might attend the meetings and vote. A majority of the shares voting was to prevail. James himself had an eighth in his own right.

Alexander prepared and published manuals, instructions for his deputy surveyors in both East and West Jersey. Copies are in the Proprietors' vault.

14 Cadwallader Colden. Like Alexander, Colden was a protégé of Argyll. *Colden*, I, 113.

Archibald Kennedy, member of N.Y. Council from April 18, 1726. He was kin to Burnet by his stepmother. *Privy Council*, III, 833.

Book for Kennedy, *Colden*, VII, 211; also *Colden*, VIII, 186-87.

Archibald Kennedy. His son returned to Scotland and became the Earl of Cassilis. Kennedy was a witness to Alexander's will many years later. During his absences, he placed his own affairs in trust with Alexander.

15 Hunter's recommendation of Alexander to Burnet. NJA, IV, 71.

16 Dunster wrote Alexander of Burnet: "Never a country was happier of a governor than these provinces are of him." He warned, however, "We may get a Pharaoh that knows not Joseph." NJA, V, 100, November, 1724.

Stephen DeLancey and his son James thus early recognized the rising fortunes of Alexander and determined to oppose them. They gathered the entire American Tory power to overthrow the young

Whig. Their activities provided him with the field of battle at law, in which he developed his political ideas. The American Tory, not its English counterpart, was the real threat to liberty and union. It was Alexander's good fortune that he managed to keep his side loyal (the "Livingston interest") to his terms.

Indian alliance and Cuyahoga grant. Governor Burnet suggested the deed, which was made by the Western Nations of New York: Seneca, Cayuga, and Onondaga. The grant is printed in NYDCH.

17 Burnet. The new governor was less interested in legal reform than in his pleasure. Alexander's attempt to reform the whole legal process in Jersey courts was disallowed by the Board of Trade. (Stevens *Index*, 153, etc.) It had been passed by the Assembly, but Burnet signed it with a disparaging comment. NJA, V, 191.

In 1741 Alexander was again made head of a committee "to inspect the various laws." NJA, III, October 16, 1741.

War at the party level. *Leder*, 282-89.

Burnet's term. An instruction was added by Lords of Trade to Governor Burnet November 23, 1723, that a suspension clause must be included in every act by legislature, before the governor should sign it. The "suspension clause" became a bone of contention, and remained so until 1776. NJA, II, 255.

Burnet. Whitehead, *Proprietary*, 160: "You seem always in a hurry"; 137: "Burnet was unrestrained with the ladies by whom he was much admired." Alexander mentioned "warmth" (hot temper) as the governor's only fault.

Governor Burnet's mother was a Dutch lady. His wife, Anna Maria Van Horne, was a cousin of Mrs. Alexander, through the Provoost connection.

Schuyler's policy. Leder, Lawrence H., "Robert Livingston: A New View of New York Politics," N.Y. *Hist.*, XL (1959), 358-67; *Robert Livingston 1654–1728 and the Politics of Colonial New York* (1961).

Marriage contract. *Fam. Rec.*, 37.

The Alexanders lived after marriage in her house on Pearl Street. They later built a residence at 66-73 Broad Street, south of Wall Street, on Lots 6, 7, and 8 in Block M of the Costello map. Stokes, *Iconography*.

18 Alexander's will made in 1745, in Peter Van Brugh Livingston's papers, NYPL, I, 81-93.

The children. The Scottish clannishness made much of godparents. In addition to Governor and Mrs. Burnet, the list gives the only direct proof of Alexander's relatives in Scotland and his own most intimate friends in his early years in America. *Fam. Rec.*, 8. They included Governor and Mrs. Burnet; John and Eva Provoost (stepson of James Alexander and his wife); Mrs. John Hamilton; John Sprat (Mrs. Alexander's half-brother); Charles Dunster; Cadwallader

Colden; Mrs. Archibald Kennedy; Patrick Graeme, Proprietor; William Alexander (brother of James), and his wife; Christian Caw and Jennet M'Crief, his sisters. The last four stood by proxies, being resident in Scotland.

Alexander family. Ruth. Coll. 1735; *N.Y. Gen. and Biog. Record,* XII, 12-15.

Mrs. Alexander shipped regularly from Curaçao in English bottoms. See *Daybook,* February 14, 1732. "Three tons of the best Esopus flour, two tons of brown bread, one ton of white bread, and 48 casks."

Mrs. Alexander. On February 2, 1753, Alexander wrote Colden, "My wife for two months past has been in a bad state of health, and continues so; but if she is able to crawl she will be in the shop. By which means she often gets fresh colds, being very tender." Alexander to *Colden,* IV, 367.

19 Country Party. Fully discussed by Mathieson in his *Union.* Alexander shared with Colden the use of the word "country."

"Our country" (meaning the New York City region). Colden, IV, 385.

Fur trade, Colden and Alexander. NYDCH, V, 726-33. Fur trade, Colden on. Smith, *History I,* 238-56 (dated November 10, 1724).

Joint paper. Report on Indians, 1724, Colden, *Five Nations,* 224-38. Smith, *History I,* 238, evidently refers to another report, signed by Walter, Van Horne, Harrison, Barberie, Colden, and Alexander, as by the two last. NYDCH, V, 982.

20 Sprat will. Rochester, N. Y., September 15, 1743. NYCM, *Alexander MSS.* (About one-half of the estate to Alexander's children, including acreage in the Paltz, at Kingston, and at New-boro [*sic*].)

Orange County purchase by Clarke, Burnet, Alexander, and Colden. NYHS *Mss,* Misc. O, May, 1722. Ruttenber, *Orange,* 121.

Purchase of Newburgh. *Colden,* I, 304; IV, 59.

Newburgh. Ruttenber, *Orange,* 122, adds that Duncan Alexander, "son of James Alexander, was also added to the list of inhabitants of Newburgh." Alexander purchased Lot 3 and was partner along with Colden in Lot 4, which was the first to bear the name. Ruttenber, *Orange,* 122–27.

The name of the city may perhaps be due to Gilbert Livingston, Sheriff of Ulster, for the first Earl of Newburgh in Scotland was James Livingston, created 1660. E. B. Livingston, *Manor Livingstons,* XXXII, 31, 32.

21 Robert Livingston and Burnet. *Leder,* 250, 251.

Livingston land title. Livingston vs. Hoffman, *Daybook,* 1742–43 includes division of Upper Nine Partners Patent; Dutchess County; purchase of Valleau's ninth share. On Livingston title, letter of April 10, 1752 NYHS, *Alexander MSS,* Box 10.

22 Archibald Kennedy, Carl Van Doren, *Franklin*, 214, 220.
Burnet as an American. NYDCH, V, 703.

Burnet's policy. Smith, *History*, 244; Alexander's letter, Colden *Five Nations*, describes the stimulus caused by Burnet's policy.

23 Mahakamak. *Colden* I, 90, June 27, 1719.
Survey of Mahakamak with *Journal*, Box 8, Alexander *Papers*.

24 DeLancey power. Twelve of 27 members of Assembly were relatives of the DeLanceys. Names and relation given. NYDH, IV, 625-37.

25 Connecticut, Massachusetts, and New York boundaries. H. N. Mac-Cracken, *Old Dutchess Forever*, 232-315.

Appointment. Chairman of commission, N.Y. Council. *Council Minutes*, December 30, 1723; *Boundaries*, II, 298-303.

Ironmasters' war. "Land Cases in Colonial New York, 1765–1767: The King vs. William Prendergast," Irving Mark and Oscar Hamlin (eds.), *New York Univ. Law Quarterly Review*, XIX, 2, January, 1942, 165-94.

Encroachment by Massachusetts, NYDCH, IV, 401.

26 Pennsylvania Line. On June 7, 1754, while Peters and Franklin were in New York, William Alexander conferred with Peters on the disputed boundary line of Pennsylvania and New York. *Alexander MSS*, NYHS.

27 Sir William Keith's application for governor of New Jersey. NYDCH, V, 446-47.

28 Disturbed eastern line. Miller, *New England Mind*, 367-70.
Ridgefield, NJA, V, 233.

29 Oblong, *Boundaries*, II, 298, 304.

Dover Treaty line, *Boundaries*, II, 255.

Alexander's program. Alexander divided his shares in the Oblong patent and in the Second Nine Partners among his children. In the Oblong, Lot 15 went to William, 4 to Elizabeth, and 64 to Anne. *Book of Deeds*, 152.

30 Population troubles. Growth of New York Province after Treaty of Dover: 1731, 50,300; 1756, 96,800. Growth of Dutchess County (including Dover): 1731, 1727; 1756, 14,000.

On October 27, 1735, five years after Chandos consulted Harrison on the prospects for African slaves, Governor Cosby filed a bill in chancery against Hawley and Company. "The child is none of mine," wrote Horsmanden bitterly. Alexander, owner of 500 acres in the Oblong, signed a petition against the bill, which was presented by L. Morris, Jr., to the N.Y. Assembly, in March, 1756. He signed also for each child's 500 acres. He and his son continued to defend the Oblong successfully.

31 Chandos affair. Andrews, *Colonial Period*, II, 230; Baker, *Chandos,*

349-53. I am greatly indebted to the Henry E. Huntington Library, San Jose, Calif., for permission to read the Chandos *Letter-books,* and to quote briefly from them. Mr. Collins Baker has graciously encouraged me to use his biography of Chandos.

The Chandos Letter-books contain the letters dated 1730–35. They have been read in photostat and microfilm. Mr. Carl M. Mishler very kindly read many of the letters, and sent me copies. He selected for me the relevant pages for the films. Vols. 44 (1733), 45 (1734), and 46 (1735) are most useful.

34 Chandos' first letter to Harrison, August 17, 1730. *Letter-book* 35; 210. Colden *Papers,* II, 23.

African company. Chandos hopes "that by God's blessing he might expect the number of slaves to increase steadily." Baker, *Chandos,* 211. It is a pleasure to learn that by 1740 he had lost £140,000 in the African company.

Chandos' offer of slaves to Harrison, *Letter-book* 35; 211.

Harrison and G. Livingston. *Leder,* 246 n., 258; Alexander, with his stepson John Provoost and a jewish neighbor, Gomez, bought out Harrison's Newburgh patent of 5,000 acres, now called Middle Hope. Ruttenber, 130. Map, p. 112.

35 Chandos' own company. He even divided up the Oblong acreage. Chandos *Letter-book,* 38; 79. Sir Joseph Eyles and his brother, Sir John Eyles, "and another gentleman," obtained 18 lots of 800 acres each; Mr. John Drummond and two others divided 16,000 acres among 20 lots; Mr. Watts for Chandos and Harrison received 19,200 acres, 24 lots; and Mr. Taylor brought up the number with 12,400 acres, 15½ lots.

36 Pope, *Epistle to the Earl of Burlington, Poems* 3, 180; 11, 107-8.

Hawley patent. *Minutes of Thos. Hawley & Co.,* in J.A.'s hand, NYHS, Box 45.

39 Hawley Co. Colden *Map on Allocation of Lots,* NYHS, Box 45.

Wrongly drawn. Alexander had discovered that Chandos had described the Oblong as lying west of the original boundary of Connecticut. It lay, of course, east of it. The error was costly, and delayed the progress of Chandos at least a year. *Colden,* November 22, 1731.

40 William Cosby, *Colden,* IX, 283-355.

Loan to Cosby. Alxeander to Collinson, letter, June 4, 1739. NJA, 1739, 71-77.

41 Suit against Rip Van Dam, Laboree, *Royal Government,* 160-64.

Cosby-Van Dam affair, Rutherfurd, *Zenger,* 17-19.

Van Dam's plea, NYDCH, V, 979.

Cosby on Alexander, NYDCH, V, 321.

Cosby urges Alexander's removal, NYDCH, V, 939-42; VI, 22, 24.

Cosby on New York. "The example and spirit of the Boston people begins to spread amongst these colonies in a most prodigious manner." Cosby to Duke of Newcastle, October 26, 1732, NYDCH, V, 937.

42 DeLancey. For a favorable view see O'Callaghan *New York;* NYDCH, IV, 625-39; *Wilson,* II, Chapter VII.

DeLancey interest, *Colden,* IX, 20.

Louis Rou, *Colden,* NYHS, 1870, "Letters on Wm. Smith."

43 Opinion, *see* Alexander, Writings.

Randolph, Sir John, NYPL, *Cosby MSS,* No. 21.

G. Clinton on Cosby under DeLancey, NYDCH, VI, 356.

Equity without consent. Alexander's case rested on the fact that the Assembly had never approved Cosby's erection of equity. The Council backed Cosby in spite of the obvious conflict of interest. The resemblance to the English Star Chamber was Alexander's chief weapon, because in both cases the head of state was party to the suit and appointed the judges.

44 Cosby on Morris, NYDCH, 4-7; 8-14.

Morris' reply to Cosby, NJA, V, 349-59, August 7, 1733.

Rashness of Morris' publication, NYDCH, V, 949.

45 Van Dam's complaint, NYDCH, VI, 8.

46 Lords to Cosby, NYDCH, VI, 42.

47 William Truesdell of Norwalk aided by Alexander. NYHS, *Alexander Papers,* I, October 23, 1733. William Truesdell was Harrison's agent to sell Chandos' leases and organize purchasers to commit riots on the Oblong. Evidence in Box 10, *Alexander Papers,* NYHS. An early purchaser of Oblong lots, he had sold 100 acres to James Brown in 1730.

48 "Incendiary Letter," *Cosby MSS,* NYPL, No. 9.

Near relatives: Mrs. Alexander was first cousin to Mrs. John Hamilton. *Jay,* 13.

49 Morris, Lewis: mission to England. His son, Robert Hunter Morris, accompanied him. For his diary, see *Penn. Magazine of History and Biography* LXIV, 164-217, 350.

Conference of Alexander, Smith, and L. Morris, Jr., to aid L. Morris, Sr. L. Morris *Papers* (1852), 22-23. Agreement of Alexander, Smith, and L. Morris, Jr., for:

1. The removal of Governor Cosby,

2. Restoration of Morris as Chief Justice,

3. The removal of Horsmanden and Harrison from Council,

4. Instructions to Cosby to pass such laws as Assembly should consider conducive to welfare of a free people; annual or triennial Assembly; Council allowed to sit without governor; governor or-

dered not to set himself above the law; new charters to New York and Albany.

New York Charter. On February 7, 1730, Mayor Lurting had made Alexander honorary freeman of City of New York in a citation for his counsel on a new charter. *N.Y. Minutes of Common Council.*

Vindication "of all the papers. . . ." Chandos *Letter-book*, 44; 316, August 5, 1734.

50 "I believe . . .", etc. Chandos *Letter-book*, 44; 343, August 12, 1734. Alexander had also retained the British legal officers, filing a caveat on the purchase, until the American company's defense could be heard. He then published the whole case of Hawley. Chandos found himself unable to cope with such legal dexterity.

51 "Poor" Palatine. The Palatine refugees from the devastating wars of Louis XIV had arrived in 1710 with Governor Hunter. The English ministry, new to the problem of settling penniless immigrants, speaking a foreign tongue, failed completely. The Palatines were scattered in the Hudson and Mohawk counties.

A photostat copy of the *New York Weekly Journal* is filed at the New York Historical Society.

Col. Morris at Eastchester. *NYWJ*, 2. Lewis Morris resigned his Assembly seat September 5, 1738.

52 Fountainhead of democracy. For the English political reformers, the best authority is William Haller, *Liberty and Reformation in the Puritan Revolution* (1955). See also G. P. Gooch, *English Democratic Ideas in the Seventeenth Century* (1898 and 1927), and Alan Simpson, *Puritanism in Old and New England,* (1963). Haller emphasizes the Scottish political thought from which Alexander drew directly.

Alexander on honor and trust. The only display of emotion in his whole writing is in a letter to Colden, on an occasion when a friend had betrayed Alexander's trust. Alexander to Colden, letter, *Papers,* I, 285, August 12, 1729.

"I would never betray a friend's secret; for neither jail nor tortures nor thousands of deaths. I may savor of Don Quixote, but they are in me deeply rooted." He wrote this "to give perspiration to the mind," his only reference to emotion.

53 Shuttle the Weaver, etc. No. 44; many others of the kind are given, including John Poor the Tenant. NYWJ, No. 45, September 9, 1744.

54 Essays on Happiness by Alexander, *Journal,* Nos. 109, 111, 145, 146. "All the world are in pursuit of it. There is no true happiness but in a virtuous and self-approving conduct."

55 Joseph Addison, "Essay on Liberty," *NYWJ*, No. 84.

56 DeLancey's choice of the two numbers, 13 and 23, containing a general accusation of endangering the safety of the province, rather than

the specific charges that involved the henchman, Harrison, was prudent. The specific acts of Cosby were too widely known to fool anybody. The dodge was too clever for a jury to swallow, for, as Colden remarked, any man of sense knew how things stood. The sum of the specific truths amounted to the truth of a general statement; the public would not be fooled or overawed.

Colden on DeLancey: "A Chief Justice known to be of an implacable temper is a terrible thing in this country." *Papers*, IX, 125.

58 Albany deed. Albany people petitioned the king against the destruction of the deed to Mohawk land by Cosby. *NYWJ*, Nos. 12 and 27, also No. 44 mentioning a caveat forbiding the granting of 50,000 acres to governor through the destruction of Albany deed. Alexander was Albany's counsel. His petition is No. 27 of Zenger *Papers*, NYPL.

A governor turns rogue, NYWJ, No. 12.

Songs from Rutherfurd. Full text in Katz. Cosby censured. In spite of the censure, the Board of Trade acquiesced in his plea to recommend Alexander's removal. They were particularly offended with Alexander and his party because they had "set up a printing press" from which he libeled the ministry. NJA, V, 409-10.

61 Alexander knew Palatines well. He was chairman of a committee of Council in 1724 which granted public lands to them at Germantown for their Lutheran Church and school. *Eccl. Rec.*, III, 2222.

63 Almost desperate. In risking trial for treason, Alexander at the same time cautiously prepared a set of endorsements by character witnesses. These are in the *Rutherfurd MSS*, II, at beginning. They include testimonials of Council of N.J. (March 18, 1735), Mayor Lurting and aldermen (March 31, 1735), Grand Jury of Middlesex County, N.J., (April 21, 1736), and Grand Jury of N.Y. (May 6, 1736).

64 Harrison convicted. He became a refugee in England. *Privy Council Acts*, III, 834; July 20, 1738.

65 Alexander disbarment, *Buranelli*, 88-91. Quotation from Alexander's complaint to Assembly Committee, 1735, 139-40.

66 The Quakers of Eastchester had been denied the vote in 1733. Alexander attacked the denial in *NYWJ*.

67 Subscription for Hamilton. *Rutherfurd Fam. Rec.*, 13. Smith's refusal to sign fortifies the probability that it was he who in advance of Zenger's trial called it a "farce." Alexander did not know the meaning of the word defeat.

Smith's "farce." *Katz*, p. 146, states that the handwriting of the *Prologue and Epilogue to the Farce* are in Alexander's hand. The library cataloger, however, suggests Smith as the author. Its cynical tone does not at all resemble Alexander's undismayed optimism. NYPL, *Zenger MSS*, No. 28.

The kind of ghosting Alexander was then engaged in may be seen in the speech delivered by Colonel Mathews before the Assembly. *Colden*, VIII, 236.

Petticoat messenger. Mrs. Alexander probably carried a complete file of the *New York Weekly Journal*, as well as Alexander's notes for the trial and his completed brief. His notes for the trial were printed by Goebel & Naughton, *Law Enforcement in Colonial New York*.

68 Libel, *Am. Jnl. Int. Law*, V, 590-607.

Truth of Libel. Delancey was perhaps in strict legality in ruling out of the trial any discussion of specific acts. Nos. 13 and 23 of the *Journal* were concerned with general conditions, reflecting on the honor of the governor. Harrison, on the other hand, burned copies of the *Journal* which charged specific offenses, chiefly his own.

70 Hamilton, Andrew. Gold box made of coins given by grateful citizens on view in Historical Society of Pennsylvania. *Penn. Magazine of History and Biography*, 1940, 300.

71 View of Zenger trial in 1814: ". . . the germ of that independence and freedom which afterwards ripened and displayed itself in securing the liberties of our country." Wm. Smith, Jr., *History of N.Y.*, ed. of 1813, 426-27 (Not by Smith at this date. The words are quoted from Gouverneur Morris).

William Livingston, NYDCH, VII, 221.

72 With the acquittal of Zenger, the accusations against Alexander also collapsed. It was, however, a mere accident that he was not removed from the Council. Lord Westmoreland, a member of the English Privy Council, prevented his dismissal by the Duke of Newcastle.

73 Alexander and Smith. Their *Complaint* was printed but never dispersed, according to *Colden*, IX, 344. Intimidated by the threat of treason, the Assembly did not act on it.

74 In April, 1735, Morris had written to Colden from London, admitting his failure to get a hearing for his cause. Colden, *Papers*, II, 135-38.

Col. Morris returned from England, NYDCH, VI, 36, 39, 40.

Nos. 31-35 of *Cosby Papers* deal with Morris-Clarke affairs.

75 Insufficient. The Lords were so amused that only Miss Vane, the susceptible mistress of the Prince of Wales, had time to listen to Morris. But His Royal Highness, being on principle in favor of morality, and therefore out of favor at court, was so far out that the best the Lords would say was that Cosby's reasons had been insufficient. Someone in authority, however, seems to have tipped off Col. Morris that if he should go home and make himself governor, he

would be indulged. Upon that hint he acted. R. H. Morris, *Diary*, NYDCH, VI, 36, 37; VII, 3.

Alexander had joined New Jersey Whigs. In the week following Cosby's death, Alexander attended the New Jersey Council. He may have taken this risk in order to push for seperate government for the province. The Council petitioned for it at their next meeting. Alexander's friends: Hamilton, Reading, Van Horne, and Farmer, composed the attendance. NJA, XIV, 521.

Charter of the city. *N.Y. Com. Council Minutes*, IV, 226. The character certificate of Alexander was signed by sixteen aldermen.

Alexander had perused and counseled on the new charter of the city. *Delafield*, II, 961.

Recipe for distemper, NYPL *Cosby Papers, Zenger MSS*, V.

76 Checks and balances, NYPL, *Cosby Papers*, No. 30.

Clarke's complaint. "It is but too manifest that juries here very rarely find for the King tho' the charge be never so well supported by evidence." Clarke's fear was echoed by Richard Bradley, attorney of New York, who wrote the Lords.

77 Triennial elections. The petition for triennial elections was often made and as often refused. NYDCH, IV, 255. Alexander's *reasons for triennial elections* in the Province of New York. NYDCH, III, 245-54. He had obtained Burnet's assent to a triennial election in New Jersey, which was, however, annulled.

Alexander and the speakership. Alexander was never a great admirer of Col. Morris. He worked loyally with his younger son, Robert Hunter Morris, and he shared the elder man's admiration of Hunter, but there is almost no reference to the Chief Justice in any of Alexander's letters or writings, although Morris in one letter addresses him as "My good friend James." Morris' dissipation, cynicism, and and masterfulnes must have offended his friend, though Alexander loyally served him in his misfortune.

78 Dignity of Assembly. In Alexander's letter to Burnet in 1729, he argued that the Assembly's power did not extend to nullify actions of the governor and Council. The latter, he argued, in its role of "advice and consent" was in effect "a cabinet council" with its equal though not superior authority.

Dignity in public offices. Alexander sought to protect the Indian nations, by moving that the Board of Commissioners be limited to nine. They must hold meetings in a grave and serious manner, not in taverns; and were to spare expense at such times. Assembly *Minutes*, October 18, 1738.

Alexander's absence from the Negro trials of 1741 is indicated by the immense amount of work carried out by the surveyor, which could not have allowed his legal services in New York. This work was fundamental to the famous *Bill of Chancery. BP*, II, 125-35.

79 Clarke's success. It is likely that Clarke bought his "indulgence" from from some of the Lords of Trade, who let him stay on after the defeat of Alexander's party. He certainly offered, through his son, 1,000 guineas to Lord de la Warre, to decline the post. In 1743 he was replaced by George Clinton, a son of the Earl of Lincoln.

81 Trade and manufacture, NYPL, *Zenger MSS*, XXX.

83 Alexander apparently boarded in Perth Amboy at Mrs. Sarjeant's inn, where the Proprietors held their meetings. He also had a house at "Toby Mills," a place I have not identified, but apparently in Orange County.

Alexander was still building his house in New York in October, 1740. NJA, VI, 107.

Until the gout struck him, he was an active commuter.

"Business to be done before going to N.J." NYHS, Papers I, 1726, folio 2. Thirty items listed.

Therapy. Alexander had protracted periods of gout at this time. Colden warned him to keep out of politics. Alexander in the ensuing years, however, attended over 200 meetings of the N.J. Council, though residing in New York.

Jews' alley, G. J. Miller, *Jewish Historical Review*, 1939, No. 35, 175-88. Alexander had frequent dealings 1722–28 with Jews both in New Jersey and New York. He drew a chancery act for the creditors of Isaac Emanuel of Freehold, 1721. One of his neighbors, named Gomez, was a partner with him in the purchase of 5,000 acres adjacent to his Newburgh patent.

Jewish friends of Alexander, *Miller*, AJHS, 35, 171-78.

Moses Franks, leading Jewish merchant, wrote Alexander from London, "I shall always be proud of your friendship." NYCM, *Alexander MSS*, July 26, 1749.

84 The youngest child, Susanna, married, after her father's death, Capt. John Reid of a Scots regiment, who returned to Edinburgh. He left an endowment to its university with the provision that an annual concert of chamber music, including his own compositions, should be given. He was an accomplished flutist. *Lochhead.*

Their daughter Susan was educated in America, but joined her father in London. She married Dr. John Robertson, a physician. Charming pictures of London society are printed by Livingston Rutherfurd from her letters to her aunt. (Printed in *Fam. Rec.*)

Municipal Library, Colden to Alexander, NJA, V, 237; Keep, *N.Y. Soc. Library*, 207; and *King*, 334.

Their eldest son, James, Jr., died young in an epidemic in 1731.

Education, *Colden*, IV, 385. Alexander also urged the education of apprentices "especially of the poorer sort." *NYWJ*, No. 170, 1737. Alexander himself took apprentices in. James Gilchrist was apprenticed to him. *Papers*, NYHS, Box 10.

85 Livingston as J. A.'s pupil. "Even at this day we extend every general
act of parliament *which we consider reasonable and fit for us,* though
it was neither designed to be a law upon us, nor has words to include
us. . . ." Wm. Livingston *Independent Reflector,* No. 12, 1753.

"It is a standing maxim of English liberty that no man shall be taxed
but by his own consent." *Ind. Reflector,* December 7, 1752. Alexander
was then selling the *Reflector* in his store, and thought highly of it.
It may well be that this was a cautionary signal that he was writing
for it.

Alexander's critique of Robert Tabor Kempe's "Moot Club" plea is
printed by Sedgwick in *William Livingston.*

86 Vesey as opponent. The assault centered in Jamaica, N. Y., where
possession of a church and parsonage, built by local tithes, was in
dispute. Alexander as attorney for the defense, won the church for
the Presbyterians. Governor Cosby then built another for the English
church. *Eccles. Rec.,* 2635-36.

Louis Rou, *see* p. 42, n.

Bought half a pew. Rev. William Vesey, Rector of Trinity Church,
New York City, was deputy for the Bishop of London over the
threatened American Establishment. *Eccles. Rec.,* 1228.

Wm. Livingston on Establishment, *Eccles. Rec.,* 3427-32; 3486;
Sedgwick *Livingston,* 93-95. Alexander's pupil introduced an act to
establish a nonsectarian college. *Eccles. Rec.,* 3523. Livingstons of
later date, 1830, interested themselves in carrying out this plan by
founding New York University. J. F. Jones, *New York University*
(1933), 22-31.

Dissent of Mr. Alexander and Mr. Smith against original charter for
King's College (1754). *Eccles. Rec.,* V, 3480.

Archibald Kennedy in his Observations (1755) favored the college as
an establishment. He wrote of Alexander's resistance to it, "This
house [the Council] has long been nibbling at the prerogative of the
Crown, for which we have had only a few gentle admonitions;
whether we may proceed so well in our attempts upon a constitutional
church and the prerogatives of the Bishops, those gentlemen of church
affairs, is what I much doubt." He sent the Ms., before printing, to
Alexander. Copy in NYPL.

William Livingston distributed throughout the province a broadside
petition for the defeat of DeLancey's plan for King's College. Dutchess
Co. Hist. Soc. *Yearbook,* 6, 52-53.

Parson Daniel Taylor ("Griffith Jenkins"). See Alexander to Thomas
Penn, *Penn Papers, Official,* IV, No. 103, Hist. Soc. of Penn. Alexander
sent a poetical "jeremiad" by Jenkins (pseudonym) to Penn for his
entertainment. *Daybook.*

Tolerance. Alexander's attitude toward sectarian quarrels probably
resembled Kennedy's, whose mother forsook the Episcopal for the

Presbyterian Church, because another lady secured the pew she wanted. Kennedy *Observations.*

87 First member in New York, Van Doren, *Franklin,* 140-41.

Edmund Halley; Duer, *Stirling,* 5.

Observatory. Alexander seems to have been the first to suggest a team of scientific observers of the transit of Mercury. "As there are now sundry nurseries of learning springing up in Pennsylvania, Jersey, New York, Connecticut, and Boston, each should provide apparatus to observe it." The transit occurred May 4th. Alexander to Franklin, January 26, 1753.

Like Franklin, Alexander took an interest in the city's daily life. He introduced street cleaning in New York. *Colden,* III, 46.

American Philosophical Society, *Colden,* I, 271 ff. The failure of Franklin's Society was due to nothing but the general indifference of Americans to cultural subjects. Alexander wrote Colden in his old age (April 15, 1753), "I am sorry to see that our country has almost got asleep and regardless of the improvement of knowledge." *Colden,* IV, 385.

88 James and Elisha Parker. Prop. Min., III, 234. Elisha was James Parker's brother. He was Franklin's successor in printing and journalism. He had a chain of newspapers, publishing in Hartford, New York, and Philadelphia. Kennedy and Franklin; Van Doren, *Franklin,* 80, 103. Franklin probably derived from Kennedy such ideas as his prediction that the American population would rise to 9,600,000 in 1870, that trade should be given more freedom, and that "liberty and encouragement are the bases of colonies" (p. 22). See also his quotation from Trenchard, "Nor will any country continue their subjection to another only because their grandmothers were acquainted." A landmark in the history of American science was passed when Alexander and his devoted friend opened and put together the new quadrant or circumferenter which had just arrived on the ship *Antelope* from London. Alexander recorded the several days of hard work which Colden and he spent on the complex instrument, before it would work. The Oxford astronomers had approved it. A new era of surveying was envisaged. N.J. Prop. Min, III, 86.

89 *Board of General Proprietors of Eastern New Jersey, Minutes.* Introduction by George J. Miller, Registrar and Editor (1949–62), 3 vols. Alexander's entries are in II, III.

Real executive. Alexander attended 255 meetings of the Proprietors during the years March, 1725, to August, 1755. He was succeeded by John Stevens. The Proprietors' "long and noteworthy career, one that is unique in the history of our country." Andrews, *Colonial Period,* IV, 180.

Dividends in Alexander's time. August 8, 1737, 2,000 acres. The New York advertisement by the Proprietors of a dividend sale of lands next the New York–New Jersey line, on March 27, 1743, no doubt aided in precipitating the boundary conflict. Dividends to present have been 27 in number, of which last four have been in cash, the latest in July, 1958. Of the earlier dividends, 19 were of "good right," and four of "Pineland right." BP, III, 234.

90 Dividends of land. At one time Alexander brought the Proprietors, as he thought, to agree to sell the whole propriety by full partition. Alexander's offer of £300 for a half share in a propriety was three times what Sir Peter Warren offered Mrs. Cosby for her Mohawk lands. *Colden*, II, 229.

Lawrie, Gawin; see Scot (Index).

92 Alexander's Bill in Chancery, *N.Y. Weekly Post Boy*, March 7, 1748. Long brief, *Daybook*, II, 16-17, 19, 23. Dutchess County.

93 Nine Partners, Second, partition by Alexander, NYDCH, VI, 29. *MacCracken* 80.

Newark, D. L. Pierson, *Narratives of Newark* (1917).

Rioters. Alexander charged the rioters with transporting Indians from David Brainerd's mission on the Delaware to frighten the quiet ones. NJA, VI, 407.

Rioters' defense, NJA, VI, 293.

Baldwin, Samuel, NJA, VI, 295.

Hampton, Jonathan, surveyor, BP, III, 327.

The people's case for Elizabeth, NJA, VI, 293.

Armed tenants. In 1756 Robert Livingston appealed to Alexander for aid against rioters on the manor. Alexander probably answered his letter of January 22 as he had answered Peters in Pennsylvania, by pointing to the resistance which his own tenants put up against such attacks. Livingston adopted the same tactics with success.

Alexander made a notable *State of Facts* to the Duke of Newcastle upon Morris' death. NJA, VI, 397-418; also to the Board, VI, 419-22.

94 Head of state. Alexander called his position "Speaker of the House of Council." NJS, 1747.

Belcher's Council. Someone in London made the "mistake" of leaving Alexander's name off the Council. His agent, Paris, called the mistake to the Board's attention. It was remedied at once, although his substitute had been elected. *Stevens*, 300.

"Tell me what to do. . . ." Belcher, *Prop.*, III, 305.

95 Neither Alexander nor the Clinker Lot seriously sought a trial. Alexander's *Bill* was an appeal to public opinion. His opponents employed his own pupils, William Livingston and William Smith, Jr., who made no serious defense. They made a well-written defense of minorities, but carefully avoided details. Its best argument was this gem: "The advantage any nation hath over another in might and power, in true religion, or in the case of government where there is

improvement of arts and sciences, doth not (with humble submission) give the nation that has these advantages in ever so great a degree, the right to the possessions of another people, be they ever so weak or unable to defend them, ever so ignorant or irreligious, ever so savage or barbarous." *Answer of Elizabeth Associates.* Extended account in N.J. Prop. Min. III, 2-240. S. Neville's speech, NJA, VI, 323-48. Proprietors' response to Wheeler's reply for rioters, NJA, VI, 367 ff.

Riots ending, NJA, IV, 552 ff.

Test case, NJA, VI, 353-61.

96 N.Y. Council. As early as 1747, Clinton had written that Alexander in New Jersey had sent more men and supplies in the campaign against Canada than had New York with twice the population. NYDCH, May 3, 1747.

Clinton said Alexander was "of much knowledge and long experience in public affairs, and thereby can be of more use to me and to any succeeding governor than any other person in this province." NYDCH, VI, 407.

N.J. *Boundary Papers,* Box 1, 217-56.

First venture, Alexander's *Journal* of East-West Jersey Line, NJA, VI, 145-49.

97 Disallowance of boundary, NYDCH, VII, 773.

Annulment of N.Y. act, June 12, 1755, NYDCH, VI, 960.

Mr. Pitt's Committee, NYDCH, VII, 773-76, June, 7, 1753.

Robert Charles, agent of Assembly. NYDCH, VII, 420.

98 Charles to DeLancey, *Boundaries,* II, 659-61.

DeLancey letter, NYDCH, VI, 829.

Proprietors' Memorial on New York aggression, NJA, VI, 297-323.

DeLancey on Temporary Line, *Boundaries,* II, 673-77, 683.

New Jersey north line, *Stevens,* 315.

Paris to Alexander, NJA, VI, 425. R. H. Morris, "government too weak." *Ibid.,* 420.

Parliamentary morality low point. The Earl of Westmoreland, leading reform Whig, accused parliamentary brokers of buying and selling seats brazenly. Hansard, *Debates,* 1745, 1322.

99 DeKey, NJA,VI, 75 ff.

The three attorneys William Livingston, William Smith, and John Morin Scott, who defended the Elizabeth Associates, also took retainers from Alexander for work elsewhere. They were called the New York Triumvirate in later times.

Committee of N.Y. *Ruth. MS,* July, 1754, 330. Alexander's entry is typical of his self-control: "Meeting at Toby Mill, February 3, 4, 1754, with Scott, Murray, McEvers. Several very impertinent things were said by Scott and McEvers which were too idle to recall."

100 Memorandum on New Jersey line by Alexander. NJA, VI, 266-97.

DeLancey lured the English with the prospect of a new "Bubble." He suggested that all New Jersey titles be abolished and then offered as a speculation. Smith, *History*, 235-38.

"Curious affair," NYDCH, IV, 686.

Belcher's gout, NJA, VIII, 142, October 9, 1755.

Ogden's answer to rioters, *Daybook*, March 25, 1756 (one week before his death).

Map of Nicolas Jan Visscher, "South River 41° 40′." NJA, VIII, 174-185. The map erroneously put Mahakamak at 41° 40′.

101 Alexander to F. J. Paris, January 3, 1755, NJA, VIII, 89-91.

Letter to F. J. Paris, NJA, V, 327-29; NYDCH, V, 942.

Alexander's proclamations to Jersey residents were printed in Franklin's paper in Philadelphia.

Disabled. Through 1754 and 1755, until September 3, he did not attend the N.J. Council. For many years his work for the Proprietors had been more pressing than that for the province, except from August, 1746, when Morris died, to 1752. Some of his absences were certainly due to gout, for Governor Morris mentions this. But Morris also mentions his friend's preference for the Proprietors. Although Morris three times, in 1740, 1742, and 1744, recommended that the Lords replace Alexander with another man, Alexander preserved the appearance of friendship. He acted as pallbearer at Morris' funeral in Morrisania. He comforted the sorrowing son, R. H. Morris, by writing him that his father could not be blamed for his latest unreasonable hostility to the New Jersey Assembly, as he was a dying man and therefore not responsible. It is possible that Morris' arbitrary conduct of affairs deterred Alexander from joining him. NJA Rolls of Attendance for years mentioned: Vols. XV and XVI.

Of Lewis Morris and his son Lewis, Colden had written long before, "I think it is the fault of the Morris family that they exhaust the subject they treat on." *Lewis Morris Papers*, 239 n.

Alexander wrote Colden of going about town in a chair; he writes in his journal of being afflicted in both feet; R. H. Morris writes of hoping to see him without crutch or cane. He was absent from 1744 to 1746, and again from August, 1752 to February, 1754. In 1755 he attended only on December 3. At other periods he was constant.

His obituary mentions a severe attack, from which he had not sufficiently recovered before hurrying to the frontier in the winter of 1756. But certainly he put out an immense amount of work from 1745 to 1756.

William Alexander's aid to his father is shown by his *Brief State of the Case Between New York and New Jersey*, with his map of the boundary, December 1, 1753. *Stevens*, 512.

New Jersey line, F. J. Paris to Jas. Alexander, R. H. Morris, *Papers,* II, No. 19, NJHS.

Paris to Board on annulment of 1755, BP, III, 295.

In 1755, Alexander was still sending Paris additional documents on the boundary. *Stevens,* 315.

102 Boundary Commission. Lords of Trade to Lords Justices, NJA, VIII, 108-10, June 5, 1755.

103 Union in 1745, *Colden,* III, 101.

104 Osborn, NYDCH, VI, 815.

105 Instructions: N.Y. Council, Privy Council *Acts,* III, 833 (February 10, 1721). N. Y. Council, *Calendar,* 281 (August 3, 1721). Montgomerie's *Instructions,* October 23, 1727: *Cosby,* III, 833; Morris (N.J.), May 18, 1738; Labaree *Royal Instructions.*

Kennedy's *Colonies,* published about this time, predicted an American population of 9,600,000 in 1870; argued for more freedom in trade.

James Alexander secured Albany lodgings for Franklin and Peters at the Congress, through his friend J. Stevenson. *Alexander Papers,* Box I, 1754. Letter of Wm. Alexander to Peters, March 30, 1754.

Pownall's plan; Gipson, *Brit. Colonies,* V, 130.

106 T. Pownall, *Considerations,* printed by J. Parker, 1756.

Pownall's proposal of a federal system for America resembled Alexander's plan of union. Schutz, *Pownall,* 210.

Alexander introduces Pownall to Peters, April 9, 1754. MS in NYCM.

Union now. In his *Review* Livingston stood with Alexander in his demand for "union now." "Without a general constitution for warlike operations we can neither plan nor execute. We have a common interest and must have a common council, *one head and one purse.*" *Review,* 162.

"I am much a stranger to politics here." *Colden,* III, 381; IV, 48-54, 1746.

Colden's comments, *Colden,* IV, 460.

107 Plan of union, Alexander *Letters,* IV, 441 ff, 460.

Alexander on Franklin's plan, *Colden,* IV, 460.

Alexander *Daybook,* July 20, 1754, "examined Plan of Union of the Colonies."

108 William Alexander at the Albany Congress got word to Col. Johnson that Connecticut was carving up the Iroquois lands, and that trouble would surely follow. Boyd, *Susquehanna,* I, 13.

Hopes of union: The Indian feeling on the eve of the war was well expressed by them to Col. Johnson, July 26, 1753, "The fine standing tree which had been planted is now leaning, being almost blown down by northerly winds." NYDCH, VI, 106-12.

Albany plan. L. H. Gipson, "Thomas Hutchinson and the Albany Plan of Union," *Penn. Magazine of History and Biography,* January, 1950, with three New England plans of union in parallel columns, pp. 28-35. All contemplate two nations, New York absorbed by New England (and New Jersey also in one plan).

Council. Alexander's friends in the N.Y. Council: Murray, Chambers, Johnson, and Smith, attended the Congress at Albany, though not so appointed by the Governor.

William Alexander was present at Albany (1754) in connection with his inheritance of Indian lands. NYDCH, VI, 880. This provided him with an excuse for attending the Conference on Indians.

109 Evans map. Alexander's concern for accurate mapping led to his strong protest against Dr. Mitchell's map of 1755 for coloring "with the New York color" the land in dispute between New York and New Jersey. August 2, 1755. N.J. Prop. Min III, 295.

The Board approved the protest, with a request "to soften and smooth it somewhat." This was Alexander's last recorded service. He was absent from the next meeting, March 14, 1756. *Ibid.,* III, 296.

110 Connecticut grants, *Boyd,* I, XXXIX, No. 157.

The Susquehanna Land Co. was formed in Connecticut to colonize Wyoming, Pa. The Delaware Co. was organized the next year to buy the land west of the Delaware River. Many settlers came, 1763–69. The Six Nations repudiated the 1754 sale, and resold to the Penns in 1768. Connecticut annexed the territory as Westmoreland Co., 1776. The Continental Congress Commission awarded the land to Pennsylvania at Trenton in 1781. After several conflicts (the Pennamite Wars) the United States Court confirmed the Pennsylvania title in 1790. O. J. Hersey, *History of Wilkes Barre;* Boyd, *Susquehanna Papers.*

Connecticut schemes for New York: *Boyd,* I, 156, 192-93, 227, *passim;* Nos. 54, 125, 143, 145, 146, on New York–New Jersey problem.

111 Wyoming (Pennsylvania), Van Doren, *Franklin,* 756-59. Franklin in 1754 made a plan to divert the Blackbirds; it had no success.

Alexander's brave resistance to the Blackbirds was admired in Pennsylvania. "We must exert the legal power we have, as the people of New Jersey have done." T. Penn to J. Hamilton, *Boyd,* IV, 308.

As late as March, 1755, James Brown met Alexander in New York to plan joint action with Pennsylvania against Connecticut. On June 25th, a certain Winchell was ejected who claimed Connecticut ownership in New Jersey. *Daybook,* 1755, 153.

On June 16, John Stevens wrote that he would try to get the foreign ringleaders arrested as "they were stirring up the Irish as well." *Daybook,* 1755.

112 Reports of committee to deal with Connecticut Blackbird settlers:

Boyd, I, 305 n; NJA, XVI, 552-55. August 20, 1755. The report advocated arrest and prosecution under New Jersey laws. "The hand of James Alexander in this report is quite obvious." *Boyd*.

The Blackbirds: *Boyd*, I, 183-318, *passim*.

Thomas Pownall, *The Administration of the Colonies* (1766), 3rd ed. Pownall on colonial opinion, Schutz, *Pownall*, 239.

"At home." Alexander in conversation so called England. N.J. Prop. Min., III, 13.

Thomas Pownall in his book refers to this custom as proof of American loyalty to the mother country.

113 Kalm visited New York in 1748. He imbibed his information from Alexander, as his praise of Burnet indicates (I, 202). He tells of securing the correct latitude and variation of compass from Alexander below. On the same page he reported the New York opinion that the colonies, in thirty to fifty years, would be "entirely independent of England" (I, 203).

"Mr. Alexander, a man of great knowledge in astronomy and mathematics, assured me . . . that on Sept. 18, 1750, the declination was . . . 6° 22′."

115 Shirley. Alexander sent his son William and pupil, Elisha Parker, to Boston about this time. It is quite possible that they were messengers to Governor Shirley. His cautionary letter quoted in text strongly suggests he was concerned in both engineering and supplies of the expedition. Shirley's later commitments to Alexander were such as to indicate a long and helpful cooperation. For an exchange of letters between William and his father, see Alexander *Papers*, Box 1, 1749–1750, Nos. 36, 40, 41, and 102. Alexander's advice shows concern to have William make a good impression on someone.

116 Shirley and G. Clinton, *Colden*, IV, 467.

Shirley's visit to New Jersey, *Daybook*, April 25-26, 1755.

Alexander persuaded New Jersey to give Shirley 500 militia to go wherever directed. NJA, VIII, 111. Massachusetts raised only 600. Also note Alexander *Daybook*, June, 1755.

N.J. Legislature. Although from Hunter's time hostile to proprietary business, the Assembly cooperated with Alexander on boundary and war issues. Thus Alexander's group led New Jersey resistance to the Stamp Act.

Shirley persuades New Jersey; *Shirley*, V, 186, 207; Alexander *Journal*, 1755.

Shirley denounced the Evans map for its use of St. Lawrence as a boundary. *N.Y. Mercury*, January 6, 1756.

117 New Jersey aid, *Gordon*, 131; NJA, XVII, 5.

Shirley and Delancey, Gipson, *British Empire*, VI, 180.

Belcher, NJA, VIII, 140. Belcher secretly suggested Alexander's removal from Council, but added, "We must leave things to time and patience." NJA, VII, 573.

118 Account of W. Alexander with P. Van B. Livingston and L. Morris (apparently as contractors for army supplies). July 29, 1757. NYHS, *Misc. MSS*, II, No. 54.

Oswego, NYDH, I, 443 ff.

Wm. Alexander, Shirley *Letters*, II, 177, May 27, 1755.

Wm. Alexander left supply firm for Shirley's staff, etc., Sedgwick, *W. Livingston*, 213-18.

Wm. Alexander drew a map of Crown Point and Montreal.

119 Joint expedition. Belcher's approval of Alexander's plan of joint expedition to Shamokin, NJA, VIII, 179. November 3, 1755. Demands regiment return, *Ibid.*, 195, December 16, 1755.

Charles Clinton; Clinton was Alexander's chief surveyor. Among other tasks, he surveyed Newark, N. J.; Chesecock Patent and Augusta tract on Jersey line; and the Second Nine Partners, Dutchess County, N. Y. NJA, VIII, 209 (1754).

Blockhouses from Mahakamak to town of Rochester in Ulster (Rondout Valley), Ruttenber, *Orange*, 54.

120 Supplies were forbidden to French colonies, at Alexander's suggestion, of course. Belcher to Assembly, February 26, 1755.

Shirley letters; Shirley *Letters*, II, 251-52; Assembly letter, 265.

House changes vote. Assembly *Minutes*; Livingston *Review*, 89.

Hardy received from Alexander full documentation on Jersey line. Belcher wrote him, "I put this in Mr. Alexander's cover to be forwarded to you, and who will at the same time furnish your Excellency with all papers in the affair." NJA, VIII, 142.

Alexander was chairman of the Council which replied loyally and gratefully to the address of Governor Sir Charles Hardy, praising his promptness in going to the front. This was on December 4, 1755. On September 11, £ 10,000 had been voted to be used in cooperation with neighboring colonies in the joint expedition planned by Alexander.

121 Pownall at Elizabeth, *Colden*, V, 24-26.

Cranberry Indians, NJA, XVI, 542, August 19, 1755.

123 Local enlistment, NJA, VIII, 92.

"battomen" (bateaux-men), *Colden*, IV, 48-51.

124 Gnadenhutten massacre, Van Doren, *Franklin*, 245.

Franklin at Easton, Van Doren, *Franklin*, 247-49.

Franklin in London. In October, 1757, Pennsylvania in vain appealed to London for aid. NJA, XVII, 163.

March to Delaware, *Colden*, IV, 48-51.

Minisink, NJA, VIII, 176-77.

125 Charles Clinton, *Colden,* V, 66.

Danger from Indians, *Colden,* V, 51.

Western frontier, R. H. Morris, *Shirley Letters,* II, 415.

Shirley on defenses: *Shirley Letters,* II, 399.

Assembly debt bills. They became a football of politics, Hardy veto-ing and DeLancey passing until DeLancey got his large increase in salary. Livingston *Review.*

Bill for expedition considered, *Daybook,* March 25, 1756.

N.Y. Assembly Acts, 1756, of March 2, April 1, May 4, etc. On December 2, 1756, an Act of Parliament was passed overriding all colonial acts dealing with the war. Probably the jockeying in New York and Sir Charles Hardy's report on it, was a principal cause of thus putting America under martial law.

Alexander's last dissent was made February 20, 1756, against the sale of land in patents on the northern boundary. He boldly stated that the Council was appropriating large sums for the benefit of three members "in this house," by which he probably meant Horsmanden, DeLancey, and Murray. He also dissented to the vote to pay sums to persons with no account of their services. He is recorded in the Minutes of the New York Council as having attended on March 26. He must have left the meeting immediately for the frontier. Savages had been reported on March 6 as invading Ulster and committing outrages at Philip Swartwout's. *Minutes of the Legislative Council,* 1250.

126 In October, 1757, while Franklin was pushing his case against Penn, the desperate Pennsylvanians appealed to the London ministry for help. They got none. Franklin, who resented both Germans and Scotch-Irish intruders, was not interested. Indians on the Juniata killed at will; among their victims was a John McCracken. NJA, XVII, 163.

Parker and Weyman, N.Y. Assembly *Minutes,* March 15, 1756.

Alexander's friends in New Jersey obtained a request "in a consti-tutional way," and gave handsomely of men and supplies to the end of the French War. *Gordon,* 131.

Goshen suffers, *Daybook,* March 25, 1756.

127 Weiser and Sir Wm. Johnson, help from General Amherst, *Boyd,* I, 129, 1762.

Alexander also prepared at this time to receive the exiled Acadians by giving them employment along the Hudson.

Johnson's treaties, Flexner, *Johnson,* 163.

William Smith states that death was due to distress over the budget bill. The *N.Y. Mercury* obituary, probably by Colden, calls it due to "zeal for the universal cause against the common enemy."

Proprietors to Mrs. Alexander, N.J. Prop. Min., III, 298.

128 *The N.Y. Mercury,* New York City, 1752–68, (continued to 1783 under the title *The New York Gazette,* and *The Weekly Mercury*).

129 Americans. General Loudon, who passed some time in New York in the fall of 1756, sized up the New York situation pretty well. "The King must trust in this country to himself, for this country will not come when he calls." He found "no law prevailing that I know of, but the rule every man pleases to lay down for himself." Letter to Governor Hardy, September 16, 1756.

The Alexander heritage of ideas was brilliantly illustrated in most of his descendants in the field of civic gifts. Dr. John Watts, a great-grandson, may stand as a type specimen. A lifelong philanthropist, his most permanent monument is the Five Points House of Industry. *Fam. Rec.,* 255.

Colden on lawyers, NYDCH, VII, 705.

130 Peter Van Brugh Livingston was a charter founder of Princeton College (1748), and was treasurer of the National Presbyterian Church. *Amer. Biog.*

William Alexander had gone to England to testify in Shirley's defense, in October, 1756. The general had begged Mrs. Alexander's permission. The courageous widow gave a vigorous approval; she felt her husband would have approved. William was aided in his quest for the title by the Marquis of Bute, Argyll's nephew. Shirley introduced William to Pitt. Shirley *Letters,* II, 481.

The Marquis of Bute was the nephew of the two Dukes of Argyll (John and Archibald). He was the favorite of George III, but was very unpopular in Parliament during 1760–62, hence he could not help Stirling to his title at that time. Bute's fall may indeed have cost Stirling the Lords' approval.

William Robertson, *Peerage* (1790), 286-87, 306-7. This gives the full minute from the House of Lords *Journal,* XXX, 186, on Alexander's petition. His agent did not dare present the evidence.

Stirling. The Duke of Argyll placed his muniment room with all its archives at William's disposal. Duer, *MSS,* NYCM.

Lord Stirling, claim; *Rogers,* 276. See also NYCM, Alexander *MSS,* letters from Andrew Stuart and H. Porteous (agents in Scotland); *Colden,* V, 159; also NYDCH, XI.

Will. James left his estate to his widow, suggesting to her that she might wish to adopt in her own will the division he would have made had she died first. William was made executor, and would have received two shares; his sisters one each; John Provoost one. David Provoost, his "son-in-law" (stepson) had died in Cartagena, 1741. His will, a substantial volume, listed his whole estate. P. Van B. Livingston's share was reduced. NYPL, Peter Van Brugh Livingston *Papers.*

Mary Alexander died in 1760. In her will she carried out her husband's suggestion. NYHS, *Abstracts of Wills,* V, 386-87; *Fam. Rec.,* 46, 47.

Having studied at the Middle Temple, as did William Franklin, he Anglicized.

130 "Gentleman Phil" Livingston. Alexander's grandson was secretary to Governor Sir Harry Moore. He was probably responsible for Moore's sending British companies to defend Livingston Manor. But in 1788, he represented Westchester at the State Constitutional Convention. A moderate Tory, he was much abroad, but had a house at Dobbs Ferry. Eberlein (1964), 15.

John Stevens' *Observations on Government* was written in reply to John Adams' *Animadversions.* Stevens followed Alexander in wanting the executive and judicial powers independent of the legislative. The pamphlet was printed in New York in 1787 by W. Ross.

Alexander's tradition of engineering is best illustrated in John Stevens, grandson, inventor, capitalist; treasurer New Jersey; colonel in militia; surveyor general. He bought land at Hoboken. Originated first patent laws of United States. He designed a multitube boiler; built the *Phoenix,* first ocean steamship.

Stevens Institute of Technology was planned by Alexander's grandson, John, and endowed by bequest of Edwin A. Stevens, great-grandson.

Robert Livingston Stevens, d. 1856. Great naval architect, designed the T-rail; bomb from cannon; yacht that beat the *America.*

Smith, *History (cont.),* 426-27. "The germ of that independence and freedom which afterwards ripened and displayed itself in securing the liberties of our country." This may indicate that Gouverneur Morris, not Richard Yates, was the author of the 1813 continuation of Smith's *History of New York,* in which these pages occur. As Smith's warm friend and former pupil, it seems probable. Morris was said to have made this remark in the Constitutional Convention.

131 The marriages of Alexander's grandchildren were a further confirmation of the strength of the family relationships with the liberal and scientific group. John Rutherfurd, his grandson, married Helena Morris, sister of Gouverneur Morris. His son, Robert Walter Rutherfurd, married Sabina Morris, daughter of Lewis Morris, the Signer. They were the parents of Lewis Morris Rutherfurd, a distinguished astronomer.

Provoost, the patriot, at Red Hook, Dangerfield, *Livingston,* 486. See also *ACB—Provoost.*

132 Wm. Alexander. Defense of Shirley, NYDCH, IV, 158-59. Alexander Colden to his father, Cadwallader Colden, on Stirling in London, 1757.

Livingston-Stirling friendship. William Alexander Livingston was killed in an army duel September 8, 1780. He was William Livingston's son.

Gouverneur Morris. His letter to Walter Rutherfurd (*Fam. Rec.*, 135-37) in December, 1789, reflects Alexander's ideas. He predicted permanency for the new federal republic because (1) there was no precedent for the failure of any real constitution; (2) the development of modern politics tended to fix the interior stability of a state; (3) an educated electorate tended to stability; (4) public justice was a great friend of an existing state; and (5) the art of printing greatly extended public stability.

John Jay's son, Peter Augustus Jay, married John Rutherfurd's sister. Alexander Hamilton spent his school days at Perth Amboy, under the Scot, Francis Barber. Morris and Duer were his intimates.

133 David Ogden, *see Genealogy of the Hoffman Family*, 491. He was judge of the New Jersey Supreme Court.

Richard Stockton, leading Jersey Constitutionalist, was an attorney for the Proprietors in 1756. He continued as counsel for years. N.J. Prop. Min., III, 351.

The Proprietors were suspended during the Revolution. Their loyalties had been divided. In September, 1784, the company was reconstituted by Alexander's heirs: Walter Rutherfurd and James Parker, two moderate loyalists, and John Stevens and his son, patriots. John Stevens became deputy surveyor general. McCormick, 238.

John Rutherfurd—N.Y. Plan. John Rutherfurd's design included a parade ground from 23rd to 34th Streets, and from Fourth to Seventh Avenues. Its only survival is Madison Square.

Worthy successors of the Bill in Chancery were John Rutherfurd's memorials and "Petitions" in 1784 to defend the Lawrence line for the eastern Proprietors. They rehearsed once more the whole history of the line from 1664. The legislature sustained Rutherfurd and Stevens, the chief agents of the Proprietors.

Bibliography

ALEXANDER MSS. IN PUBLIC LIBRARIES:

It would be a task beyond this writer's powers to give a complete bibliography of Alexander, because of the nature of his profession and the abundance of material. A list of the principal centers where source material may be found follows.

NEW YORK:

New York Historical Society: 69 boxes of uncataloged material, chiefly allocated to counties in New York and New Jersey. Folio volumes: Cadwallader Colden Papers. Letters to Dr. Colden from James Alexander and others.

New York Public Library: Cosby Papers; Zenger Papers.

Museum of the City of New York: Alexander MSS. (especially of William Alexander).

New York State Library, Albany, New York: Calendars of official acts. Council records.

NEW JERSEY:

New Jersey State Library
Office of the State Archivist
Supreme Court Records

Perth Amboy (City Hall): Office of the Board of General Proprietors of East New Jersey, George J. Miller, Registrar; Circular of Materials of the Board; Warrants, surveys, deeds, maps, etc. (over 100,000 items); Bound volumes of the same.

Minutes of the Board, three volumes, edited by G. J. Miller. Prepared in great part under Alexander's direction, often in his own hand. Only the *Minutes* have been printed: I (1685–1705); II (1725–1744); III (1745–1764). Alexander is credited with the revival of the Company in 1725. The Minutes bear this out.

New Jersey Historical Society: Rutherfurd MSS. Collection; Many documents printed in New Jersey Archives; Folio volumes (in library catalog).

ALEXANDER, JAMES, WRITINGS OF (principally on public affairs), a selection:

1712–1713—*Journal of Voyage of H. M. S. Arundel.* NJHS, MS.

1719—*Journal Kept by James Alexander During His Execution of the Commission for Running the Division Line Between the Province of New Jersey and the Province of New York.* NYHS, Alexander *Papers,* Box 10.

1720—*The Inventory of my Stock, containing what I have in many lands and debts owing me, and also what debts are due by me to others.* NJHS, Rutherfurd *MSS.*

Indian treaties, edited, 4 vols. folio (now lost). N.Y. State Library.

1720–1755—Letters to Cadwallader Colden. NYHS, Colden *Papers* I-IX.

1721—"further reasons for passing the act making current £40000 in bills of credit 12 May, 1721." NJA, V, 94-96.

Report of Alexander as Attorney General on running division line between Orange and Ulster Counties October 9, 1721. N.Y. Council *Cal.,* 282.

1721–1745—*Docket of Cases in the Supreme Court of New York, and the Mayor's Court of the City, 1721–1745.* NYHS, Alexander *Papers,* Box 10.

1724—"Report on Albany Trade, 1724," [with Colden]. Printed in Colden, C., *The History of the Five Nations.*

A law for reducing the delays of suits in the law courts, which at the time clogged every court in New Jersey. See Stevens, Henry, *Index.*

1726—On the advantage (and disadvantage) of levying duties by New York; NYHS, Colden *Papers,* IX, 267 f. Pamphlets, anonymous, perhaps a joint product of Colden and Alexander.

1727—*Law Reforms for Obtaining Survey Warrants.* NJB Prop. Vault.

1728—*Paper on the Court of Chancery* (September 1, 1728). NYHS, Colden *Papers,* I, 263-69.

1729—*The Relative Power of the Plantation Assemblies.* NJA, V, 230-33, January 27, 1729 (letter to Governor Burnet).

1732—*Journal of the Oblong Company.* NYHS, Alexander *Papers,* Box 45.

1733—"Advertisement" of the case of Thomas Hawley and Company.

Arguments of the Counsel for the Defendant, in Support of a Plea to the Jurisdiction against Rip Van Dam.

1734—*Some Observations on James DeLancey's Charge to the Grand Jury* [with Wm. Smith].

Heads of Articles of Complaint by Rip Van Dam, Esq., Against His Excellency William Cosby, Governor of New York.

The Vindication of James Alexander and William Smith from the Matters Charged in Two Pamphlets by the Hon. Francis Harrison and the Report of the Committee of Council with a Brief Report of the Case of William Truesdell Against Francis Harrison.

Mr. Smith's Opinion, humbly offered to the General Assembly of the Colony of New York, on the 7th of June, 1734, at their request. Occasioned by sundry petitions of the inhabitants of the City of New York, Westchester County, and Queens County to the said General Assembly, praying an establishment of courts of justice within the said colony by act of the legislature.

1735—Brief for Zenger (not found unless identical with notes for brief "30 folio pages," 117).

Notes for brief. Rutherfurd MSS, II, 35; Goebel, J. 782-86; and Katz, S. N., 139-45.

The Complaint of James Alexander and William Smith to the Committee of the General Assembly of the Colony of New York, and Minutes of the Supreme Court Setting Aside the Rule.

1736—*The Trial of John Peter Zenger,* edited in modernized edition by Vincent Buranelli (1957).

A Brief Narrative of the Case and Trial of John Peter Zenger, Printer of the New York Weekly Journal by James Alexander. Edited by Stanley Nider Katz, 1963.

1737—Letters on Free Speech, *Pennsylvania Gazette; New York Weekly Journal;* and Katz, S. N.

1738—*Reasons in Support of Triennial Elections in the Province of New York.* O'Callaghan, E. B., NYDH, III.

1741—Law reform on recording deeds and mortgages, also on estate of femme court, by conveyance. October 20-21, 1741. NJA, XV, 211 ff.

1741-1742—*Diary 1741-1742.* NYHS, Misc. MSS, Box 10, Sect. 2.

1742-1752—*Second Nine Partners Patent.* NYHS, Alexander *Papers,* Boxes 62, 63.

1745—*Will* of James Alexander. NYPL, Peter Van B. Livingston *Papers.* (Witnessed by both Archibald and Mary Kennedy, and by Evert Bancker.)

1746—*General Instructions of the Surveyor General to the Deputy Surveyors of the Eastern Division of New Jersey.* NYPL, Rare Book Room.

State of Facts, from September 19, 1745, to December 8, 1746 (to the Duke of Newcastle) [with R. H. Morris]. NJA, IV, 397-418.

Publication of Proprietors of East Jersey, March 25, 1746. NJA, VI, 292-323.

Chronicles of Disorders in New Jersey

1747—Petition (of Proprietors) against change of New York–New Jersey line. NJA, VIII, 160-81, 202-44.

A Bill in the Chancery of New Jersey at the Suit of John Earl of Stair and Others Proprietors of the Eastern Division of New Jersey Against Benjamin Bond and Some Other Persons of Elizabethtown Distinguished by the Name of the Clinker Lot Right Men with Three Maps Done from Copper Plates to which Is Added the Publication of the Proprietors of East New Jersey and Mr. Nevill's Speeches to the General Assembly Concerning the Riots Committed in New Jersey and the Pretences of the Rioters and their Seducers. Published by subscription, printed by James Parker. (The famous "Bill in Chancery.")

1750—"Advice to John Tabor Kempe." Printed in Sedgwick, T., *A Memoir of the Life of William Livingston.*

Proposed instruction from the Lords of Trade, setting up a stronger police in New Jersey. NJHS, R. H. Morris *Papers,* No. 14, 7-9, 10-12.

1750, 1752, 1754–1756—*Daybooks.* NJHS Collection.

1752—*Memorial* of N.J. Proprietors to Pitt Report.

1753—*Thoughts for York Assembly.* NJHS, R. H. Morris *Papers* II, 1-3, December 1, 1753. (A defense of New Jersey line of 1717.)

1754—*Legal Instructions for Young Attorneys.* NJB Prop. Vault.
Simplified Instructions to Attorneys in Making Evictions Just and Peaceable. NJB Prop. Vault.

Directions Where Lands Are Taken Up Upon Rights, Which Lands Were Never Before Duly Taken Up and Recorded. Daybook 1754, inserted leaf March 13 at p. 351. (Five steps listed.)

Thoughts on Leets and Lodges (Briefs and Complaints). (Mentioned in *Daybook.*)

MISCELLANEOUS:

American Constitution. NYPL, Zenger, J. P., *A-Z Papers.*

Recipe for Distemper in Body Politic. NYPL, Zenger, J. P., *A-Z Papers.*

Letters to Thomas Penn, *Pennsylvania Magazine of History and Biography,* Vol. 16, 26-27; William Alexander, Benjamin Franklin, R. H. Morris, David Ogden, William Shirley, John Stevens.

Andrews, C. M., *The Colonial Period of American History* (1937).

Arts and Crafts in New York 1726–1776, The (1938). NYHS.

A-Z Papers, New York Public Library, Manuscript Division, Cosby *MSS.* and Zenger *MSS.*

Boundaries of the State of New York, Report of the Regents of the University, 2 vols. (1872).

B. Prop. See *Board of Proprietors.*

Boyd, J. P., *Susquehanna Papers* (1938).

Calendar of New York Colonial Commissions, edited by Edmund B. O'Callaghan (1929).

Campbell, Alexander, *Protestation* (1733).

Chandos, Duke of, *Letter-books,* Henry E. Huntington Library, San Marino, California.

Colden, Dr. Cadwallader, *The History of The Five Nations of Canada, Which are Depending on the Province of New York in America, and Are the Barrier Between the English and French at that Part of the World,* 2 vols., third edition (1755); *History of Gov. Cosby's Administration,* NYHS, Pubs. Vol. IX; *Papers,* NYHS, Vols. I-IX: I-II, 1876–77; III-VII, 1917–23; VIII-IX, 1934–35.

Colden, Cadwallader, *The Colden Letters on Smith's History,* NYHS Colls. 1868; 1869.

Collins Baker, C. H., and Muriel L., *The Life and Circumstances of James Brydges, First Duke of Chandos, Patron of the Liberal Arts* (1949).

The Colonial Laws of New York from the Year 1664 to the Revolution, 5 vols. (1894).

Dangerfield, George, *Chancellor Robert R. Livingston of New York* (1960).

Delafield, General John Ross, *The Family History* (1945).

Delafield, Maturin L., "William Smith, Jr., the Historian," *Magazine of American History* (1881).

DeLancey, James, *Sentiments of a Principal Freeholder* (1738). NYPL Cosby *MSS.*

Duer, William Alexander, *Life of William Alexander Lord Stirling* (1847).

Eberlein, Harold D., and Hubbard, C. Van Dyke, *Historic Houses of the Hudson Valley* (1942).

Eusden, John, *Puritan Lawyers and Politics in Early Seventeenth Century England* (1958).

Evans, Lewis, *Geographical, Historical, Political and Mechanical Essays* with map (1755).

Fish, Stuyvesant, *Pedigree,* etc.

Fisher, Edgar J., *New Jersey as a Royal Province* (1911).

Gipson, Lawrence H., *The British Empire Before the American Revolution,* 9 vols. (1936–56).

Goebel, Julius, Jr., and Naughton, T. R., *Law Enforcement in Colonial New York* (1944).

Gooch, George P., and Laski, Harold J., *English Democratic Ideas in the Seventeenth Century* (1954).

Gordon, Thomas F., *The History of New Jersey, from Its Discovery by Europeans, to the Adoption of the Federal Constitution* (1834).

Haines, Charles G., *The American Doctrine of Judicial Supremacy* (1914).

Hamilton, Andrew (descendant), *The Life of Andrew Hamilton Daystar of the American Revolution* (1940).

Harrison, Francis, *Letter to the Council on the Report of Committee on the Incendiary Letter,* NYHS *Colls.* (1935).

Hatfield, Edwin Francis, *The History of Elizabeth, New Jersey* (1868).

Holdsworth, Sir William S., *A History of English Law,* 10 vols. (1922–1938).

Independent Reflector, published by William Livingston. December 7, 1752.

Insh, George P., *Scottish Colonial Schemes* (1922); *The Scottish Jacobite Movement* (1960).

Jay, Elizabeth Clarkson, "Descendants," *N.Y. Genealogical and Biographical Record,* XII.

Johnson, Sir William, *An Account of Conferences Held and Treaties Made Between Major General Sir William Johnson, and the Chief Sachems of the Mohawks and (13 Other Nations) in the Years 1755 and 1756.* London (1756).

Journal of the Legislative Council of . . . New York, 2 vols. (1861).

Journal of the Votes and Proceedings of the General Assembly of the Colony of New York, 3 vols.

Journals of the House of Lords, XXX, 186.

Kalm, Per, *Travels in North America,* edited by A. B. Benson, 1937, II; at Alexander's house 1748.

Katz, Stanley Nider, *A Brief Narrative of the Case and Trial of John Peter Zenger, Printer of the New York Weekly Journal, by James Alexan-*

der (1963). (Katz prints as Alexander's *Prologue and Epilogue to the Farce*. It is not here included as genuine.)

Keith, Sir William, *A Short Discourse upon the Present State of the Colonies in America in Respect to the Interest of Great Britain* (1728). NJA, V, 215-30.

Kennedy, Archibald, *Observations on the Importance of the Northern Colonies to Great Britain under Proper Regulations* (1750) NYPL; *Serious Considerations on the Present State of Affairs* (1754) NYPL; *Speech by a Dissenting Member of the Church* (1755) NYPL.

King, Marion, *Books and People* (1954). (History of N.Y. Society Library.)

Knollenberg, Bernard, *Origin of the American Revolution: 1759–1766*, (1960).

Labaree, Leonard W., *Royal Instructions to British Colonial Governors in America*, 2 vols. (1935).

Lawrie, Gowan, *Brief Account, etc., 1686*, edited by J. E. Pomfret, NJHS, V 75.

Leder, Lawrence H., *Robert Livingston and the Politics of Colonial New York* (1961).

Lincoln, Charles H., *Correspondence of William Shirley, 1731–1760*, 2 vols. (1912).

Livingston, E. B., *The Livingstons of Livingston Manor*, 1.

Livingston, Peter Van B., *Papers*, NYPL.

Livingston, William, *A Letter to the Right Reverend Father in God, John Lord Bishop of Landaff . . . etc.* (1768); *A Review of the Military Operations in North America from the Commencement of the French Hostilities on the Frontiers of Virginia in 1753, to the Surrender of Oswego, on the 14th of August, 1756, in a Letter to a Nobleman* (1756); "Watchtower" in *New York Mercury* (November 17, 1755).

Livingston, William, and Smith, William, Jr., *An Answer to the Council of Proprietors*. Two publications set forth at Perth Amboy March 21, 1746, and March 25, 1747. New York, printed and sold by the Widow Catherine Zenger, 1747 (13 pp.) Rutherfurd, L., *Zenger*, 167.

Lochhead, Marion, *The Scots Household in the Eighteenth Century* (1948).

Macadam, D., *History of the Bench and Bar of New York* (1897).

MacCracken, H. N., *Old Dutchess Forever* (1958).

MacKenzie, Agnees M., *Scotland in Modern Times* (1942)

Mathieson, William Law, *Scotland and the Union, a History of Scotland from 1695 to 1747* (1905).

McAnear, Beverly, "An American in London," *Pennsylvania Magazine of History and Biography*, vol. 64, 164-217. (Robert Hunter Morris in London 1749–53.)

Miller, George J., *James Alexander and the Jews*, Am. Jewish Hist. Society, 1939, No. 35, 171-88.

Miller, Perry, *From Colony to Province* (1937).

Minutes of the Board of Proprietors of Eastern New Jersey, edited by George J. Miller, 3 vols. (1949–60).

Morris *Papers*. Collection of Documents in New Jersey Historical Society, Newark, N. J. For R. H. Morris, see "An American in London," *Pennsylvania Magazine of History and Biography*, LXIV, 164-217, 350.

New York City Common Council Minutes (1730).

New York Gazette, The, New York City, published by William Bradford (1726–44); published by William Weyman (1759–67).

New York Gazette, or *Weekly Post-Boy* (or similar name), New York City (1747–73).

New York Mercury, New York City, 1752–68. (Continued to 1783 under the title *The New York Gazette; and the Weekly Mercury*.)

New York Weekly Journal (photostat NYHS), New York City published by John Peter Zenger (1733–51).

New York Weekly Post-Boy (1743–47).

NJA—*Archives of the New Jersey Historical Society*. (1) *Documents Relating to the Colonial History of the State of New Jersey*, I-VII, edited by William A. Whitehead (1882–86); (2) *Minutes of the Governor's Council of New Jersey*, XIV-XVII, edited by Frederick W. Ricord and William Nelson (1880–86).

NJB Prop. Min.—*The Minutes of the Board of Proprietors of the Eastern Division of New Jersey*, 3 vols.: I, 1685–1705; II, 1725–44; III, 1745–64 (1949–62).

NJB Prop. Vault—Papers of the Board of Proprietors of the Eastern Division of New Jersey.

NJHS—New Jersey Historical Society.

Notestein, Wallace, *The Scot in History* (1947).

NYCM—Museum of the City of New York.

N.Y. Council *Cal.*—*New York Calendar of Council Minutes*, 1668–1783.

NYDCH—*Documents Relative to the Colonial History of the State of New York*, collected by John Romeyn Brodhead, edited by Edmund B. O'Callaghan, 15 vols. (1853–87).

NYDH—*The Documentary History of the State of New York*, edited by Edmund B. O'Callaghan, 4 vols. (1849–51).

N.Y. Eccles. Recs.—*Ecclesiastical Records of the State of New York*, vols. 3 to 5, page numbering consecutive in 7 volumes (1901–16).

NYHS—New York Historical Society. (Alexander *MSS.* and *Papers*).

NYPL—New York Public Library.

NYWJ—*New York Weekly Journal* (1733–38).

O'Callaghan, Edmund B., *Memoirs of the Honorable James DeLancey*, NYDH, IV, 625-39 (1849).

Osgood, H. L., *The American Colonies in the Eighteenth Century*, 4 vols. (1924).

Paltsis, V. H., *Bulletin N. Y. Public Library* 2, 249-55; 44, 523-27; Cosby *MSS;* Zenger *MSS*.

Pargellis, Stanley, *Military Affairs in North America, 1748–1765* (1936).

Pennsylvania Gazette (1737).

Pomfret, John E., *The New Jersey Proprietors and Their Lands, 1664–1776*. New Jersey State Library *MS* (not circulated in press).

Pope, Alexander, "Epistle to the Earl of Burlington," *Poems,* edited by William Courthope.

Poughkeepsie Journal, Poughkeepsie, N. Y., December 8, 1963. See Helen Myers.

Pownall, Thomas, *The Administration of the Colonies* (1766).

Privy Council of England, Acts of the, vols. II-IV (1720–57).

Provoost, A. J., *Biographical and Genealogical Notes of the Provoost Family,* 1545–1893 (1895).

Remarks on the Trial of John Peter Zenger, Written by Two Eminent Lawyers in One of the Colonies in America (1738); in Katz, S. N., Zenger. (Barbados.)

Report of the Regents of the University on the Boundaries of the State of New York, 2 vols. (1874, 1884).

Robbins, Caroline, *Eighteenth Century Commonwealthmen* (1959).

Robertson, William, *Scots Peerage* (1790).

Rogers, Rev. Charles, *Memorials of the Earls of Stirling and House of Alexander* (1878).

Rutherfurd (Scots jurist), *Lex Rex* (1703).

Rutherfurd *MSS.* Collection of Documents in New Jersey Historical Society, Newark, N. J.

Rutherfurd, Livingston, *Family Records and Events.* . . . (1894); *John Peter Zenger, His Press, His Trial, and a Bibliography of Zenger Imprints. Also a Reprint of the First Edition of the Trial* (1904).

Ruttenber, E. M., *History of the County of Orange,* with a history of the town and city of Newburgh (1875).

Sabine, Lorenzo, *Biographical Sketches of Loyalists of the American Revolution with an Historical Essay,* 2 vols. (1864).

Sabine, William H. W., *Historical Memoirs from 16 March, 1763, to 9 July, 1776, of William Smith, Historian of the Province of New York.* . . . (1956).

Schutz, John A., *Thomas Pownall, British Defender of American Liberty* (1951); *William Shirley, King's Governor of Massachusetts* (1961).

Scot, Robert, *Model of the Government of East Jersey* (1685).

Sedgwick, Theodore, *A Memoir of the Life of William Livingston, with Extracts from His Correspondence* (1833).

Shepard, William, *The Touchstone of Common Assurances* (1648).

Shirley, William, *Correspondence of William Shirley,* edited by C. H. Lincoln, 2 vols. (1912).

Smith, William, Jr., *Historical Memoirs to 1783,* 6 vols. NYHS *MS.; The History of the Province of New York from the First Discovery to the Year MDCCLVII* (1757), with continuations after 1762 (1815, 1823), (1729 to 1762 by W. S.), (1756, 1762, 1815, 1823).

"Smith, William, Sr.," *Mag. Am. Hist.* (1881).

Smith, William, Sr., *Prologue and Epilogue to the Farce,* Zenger MSS, NYPL.

Stevens, Henry S., *An Analytical Index to the Colonial Documents of New Jersey in the State Paper Offices of England* (1858).

Stevens, John, *A Concise View of the Controversy* (1785); *Observations on Government* (1787).

Stevens, John II, Pamphlet on the *U.S. Constitution.*

Supreme Court of Judicature of the Province of New York, The, 1691–1704, edited by Paul M. Hamlin and Charles E. Baker (1959).

Tanner, Edwin Pratt, *The Province of New Jersey* (1908).

Taylor, Rev. Daniel, *Brief Vindication of the Purchasers Against the Proprietors in a Christian Manner.* NJA VI, 266-92. Griffith Jenkins, Pseud.

Trenchard, John, with Gordon, Thomas, *Cato's Letters; or Essays on Liberty, Civil and Religious and Other Important Subjects* (London, 1723).

Trial of John Peter Zenger, The, edited by Vincent Buranelli (1957).

Van Doren, Carl, *Benjamin Franklin* (1938).

Volwiler, Albert T., *George Croghan and the Westward Movement 1741–1782* (1926).

Wallace, Paul A. W., *Conrad Weiser 1696–1760. . . .* (1945).

Whitehead, William A., *Contributions to the Early History of Perth Amboy* (1856); "East Jersey Under Proprietary Governments," *New Jersey Historical Society Collections* (1846–75); *The Papers of Lewis Morris, Governor of the Province of New Jersey from 1738 to 1746* (1852).

Wilson, J. G., *Memorial History of New York City* (1892–95).

Index

INDEX A